For two thousand years the church has had to defend doctrinal truth and oppose theological error. Now, in a stunning historical deve  in Christian history we have to define and defend basic issues of sex and gender. The Bible begins w beings as male and female. Now, we are in the position of arguing for the truth of creation itself. Denny Burk, David Closson, and Colin Smothers offer biblical insight and clarity in this important study. This study is theologically solid and incredibly timely.

R. Albert Mohler, Jr.
President, The Southern Baptist Theological Seminary

We live in a time where we, as Christians, constantly face opposition in our culture. One of the most contested topics is love: the definition of marriage, what the Bible says about homosexuality, and even the roles of a husband and a wife. This timely Bible study is needed in a time such as this. I'm thankful that *Male and Female He Created Them* is a sound yet simple theological study that takes you back to the basics of the Bible. It's a great challenge to Christians to know what God's Word says to help us clearly define what we believe and why we believe it.

Cissie Graham Lynch
Senior Advisor and Ministry Spokesperson for the
Billy Graham Evangelistic Association and Samaritan's Purse,
Host of the Fearless with Cissie Graham Lynch podcast

We live in morally confused times. Nowhere is that more obvious than in our culture's approach to marriage and sexuality. Unfortunately, the church has too often been on the sidelines when it comes to discipling believers on these topics and our nation has suffered as a result. God calls us to think biblically about everything, including sexuality, and I'm grateful for this resource and how it equips Christians to think faithfully on these contested issues.

Tony Perkins
President, Family Research Council

Male and Female He Created Them will become the most sought out and important book study for churches in the coming days. It meets our most profound need: understanding that men and women, created by God, are not interchangeable, and therefore, our callings in this world are neither arbitrary nor constraining. This study does the heavy lifting: it defines terms and situates them in a biblical worldview, and simultaneously reads the culture's idols under submission to the

Word of God. This study is deeply pastoral, recognizing that the saints who will read and use this book are not outsiders. We all have loved ones trapped in the idolatry of sexual identity, or we once were stuck there ourselves. This study will be a lifesaver for parents and grandparents of prodigals, helping us to have compassion without falling for indoctrination. I cannot recommend it highly enough.

Rosaria Butterfield
Author of *The Gospel Comes with a House Key*
and *The Secret Thoughts of an Unlikely Convert*

What an extraordinary resource so urgently needed at this time. I am happy to commend what Burk, Smothers, and Closson have put together in *Male and Female He Created Them*. Churches, community groups, and discipleship groups will be strengthened to know what the Bible teaches on controversial topics in our culture, but also be given the ability to explain why we believe these truths are the only pathway for humanity to find temporal and eternal blessing.

Andrew T. Walker
Associate Professor of Christian Ethics
The Southern Baptist Theological Seminary and Fellow,
the Ethics and Public Policy Center

MALE & FEMALE

HE CREATED THEM

A STUDY ON GENDER, SEXUALITY, & MARRIAGE

Denny Burk, David Closson, & Colin Smothers

CHRISTIAN
FOCUS

Copyright © 2023 Denny Burk, David Closson, & Colin Smothers

Paperback ISBN: 978-1-5271-0974-2
ebook ISBN 978-1-5271-1026-7

Published in 2023
by
Christian Focus Publications Ltd,
Geanies House, Fearn, Ross-shire,
IV20 1TW, Scotland, UK.
www.christianfocus.com

Cover design by Daniel van Stratten/Lifeway

Printed by Bell and Bain, Glasgow

Contents

About the Authors

Denny Burk is a professor of Biblical Studies at Boyce College, which is the undergraduate school of The Southern Baptist Theological Seminary in Louisville, Kentucky. He also serves as one of the preaching pastors at Kenwood Baptist Church. His academic interests have focused on sexual ethics and the Bible. In 2013, he published a book on sexual ethics titled *What Is the Meaning of Sex?* (Crossway). He followed that in 2015 with a book titled *Transforming Homosexuality: What the Bible Says about Sexual Orientation and Change* (P&R). He serves as the President of the Council on Biblical Manhood and Womanhood, which is a ministry that provides biblically-based resources on sexuality and gender (CBMW.org).

David Closson serves as the Director of the Center for Biblical Worldview at Family Research Council where he researches and writes on life, human sexuality, religious liberty, and related issues from a biblical worldview. His writing has appeared at Fox News, National Review, Real Clear Politics, The Council for Biblical Manhood and Womanhood, The Gospel Coalition, Townhall, 'Decision Magazine', and 'Christian Post'. David is a regular guest on Washington Watch, FRC's national television and radio program heard on over 800 stations in forty-eight states. Currently, David is completing a Ph.D. in Christian Ethics at Southwestern Baptist Theological Seminary. David is a graduate of The Southern Baptist Theological Seminary (M.Div., Th.M.) and the University of Central Florida. David lives in Washington, D.C. and is a member of Capitol Hill Baptist Church.

Colin Smothers serves as the Executive Director of the Council on Biblical Manhood and Womanhood (CBMW) and Director of the Kenwood Institute at Kenwood Baptist Church in Louisville, Kentucky. He also teaches adjunctly for Boyce College. Colin is the Executive Editor of *Eikon*, CBMW's academic journal. He has written a number of essays and articles on issues related to gender, sexuality, and the family, and is the author of *In Your Mouth and In Your Heart: A Study of Deuteronomy 30:12-14 in Paul's Letter to the Romans in Canonical Context* (Pickwick, 2022), which is based on his Ph.D. dissertation completed at The Southern Baptist Theological Seminary. Colin and his wife Elise have five children.

How to Use this Book

*This Bible study book includes 8 weeks of
content for group and personal study.*

This book is designed for group settings such as Sunday school classes or small group Bible studies,
but it can also be done individually. The chapter outline is as follows:

- Creation's Warrant: Reasoning 'From the Beginning'
- Creation's Order: Sex, Gender, Nature, and Marriage
- Sin's Disorder: Exchanging the Truth of God for a Lie
- Temptation, Desire, and Orientation
- Transgenderism
- Intersex
- Identity and Sanctification
- Sexual Sin and the Gospel

Chapter 1 starts with a group session (no individual study). All other sessions start with an
individual study followed by a group discussion.

It is recommended that participants complete the individual study before the group meets.
The individual study begins with a few pages of content designed to orient readers to the lesson's
topic. Next, there is a page for journaling and reflection. After the journaling page, there is a
'Conversation Guide' that addresses a different aspect of the issue. These guides include sermon or
book excerpts selected to reinforce the lesson's main point.

The group study begins with some interactive questions followed by additional content.
Auxiliary resources to this book can be found at http://hecreatedthem.org/ including multimedia
resources that can aid group discussion and individual study. Leaders can use the questions
scattered throughout the chapters to facilitate discussion (answers are provided in the Conversation
Guides which appear at the end of each chapter). Each lesson concludes with a weekly reflection,
recap of main points, application questions, and a memory verse.

Conversation Guide

HOW TO USE THE CONVERSATION GUIDE

The Conversation Guide is designed to help the group facilitator lead discussion. After lesson 1 (which does not contain an individual study), each lesson is divided into an individual and group study. In the group portion, there is a mixture of content and questions. These questions are designed to spark conversation among the members of the group.

However, we recognize that some of the content in our study is challenging and not everyone is up to speed on transgenderism, disorders of sex development (such as intersex), and some of the other topics covered in the curriculum. The Conversation Guide provides succinct answers to the group study questions. These answers appear in everyone's book and could be used as a starting place for answering questions that come up during the lesson.

Week 1
CREATION'S WARRANT
REASONING 'FROM THE BEGINNING'

Watch

Follow along as you watch the video for Session 1.

This page is provided for you to take notes as you watch the video.

Group Experience

From the beginning it was not so.
MATTHEW 19:8

Whenever Jesus or the apostle Paul quotes the Old Testament about the meaning of marriage and human sexuality, they never appeal to the examples of polygamist kings like David or Solomon. Nor do they invoke the examples of polygamist patriarchs like Abraham, Isaac, or Jacob. Despite the important roles that these men played in the biblical storyline, Jesus and Paul never used any of them as a model when defining what marriage is. Instead, Jesus and Paul always appeal to the pre-Fall union of Adam and Eve—a one-flesh, covenantal union of one man and one woman. This is the lone example in the Bible of a sexual and marital union that was without sin and totally according to God's design. For this reason, it is this first marriage that Jesus and Paul set forth as the paradigm for all marriages that follow. Indeed, in Jesus' teaching about divorce, He confronts the Pharisees' mistaken views about marriage by invoking that first marriage: 'from the beginning it was not so...'

In Matthew 19, the Pharisees try to trap Jesus by baiting Him into contradicting the Old Testament. The question they pose to Him is narrowly focused on whether divorce is lawful. But Jesus' reply has implications far beyond divorce and marriage. His answer gets to the heart of God's will for creation and provides an example of how to use the Bible to understand God's original design for humanity.

Take a moment to read Matthew 19:3-9

And Pharisees came up to him and tested him by asking, 'Is it lawful to divorce one's wife for any cause?' He answered, 'Have you not read that he who created them from the beginning made them male and female, and said, "Therefore a man shall leave his father and his mother and hold fast to his wife, and the two shall become one flesh"? So they are no longer two but one flesh. What therefore God has joined together, let not man separate.' They said to him, 'Why then did Moses command one to give a certificate of divorce and to send her away?' He said to them, 'Because of your hardness of heart Moses allowed you to divorce your wives, but from the beginning it was not so. And I say to you: whoever divorces his wife, except for sexual immorality, and marries another, commits adultery.'
MATTHEW 19:3-9

As Christians, we believe the Bible has all the answers to life's big questions. When it comes to questions related to marriage and human sexuality, do you look to the Bible for answers? Do you know where to look to learn about God's plan for marriage and sexuality?

How does Jesus answer the Pharisees' question in Matthew 19? Specifically, how does He use Old Testament Scripture to point to something even deeper than what they asked Him about?

What is Jesus referring to when He says, 'but from the beginning it was not so'? How does Jesus' use of Scripture help us understand God's original plan for the created order?

Note where Jesus directs the Pharisees in His answer about whether divorce is lawful. Jesus refers them back to the beginning, to the first two chapters of Genesis. Compare Matthew 19:4 and Genesis 1:27:

Have you not read that He who created them from the beginning made them MALE AND FEMALE?	So God created man in His own image, in the image of God he created him; MALE AND FEMALE he created them.
MATTHEW 19:4	**GENESIS 1:27**

PRINCIPLE: *When reading and interpreting the Bible, remember that Scripture helps us interpret Scripture.*

After directing the Pharisees' attention to Genesis 1:27, Jesus quotes Genesis 2:24: 'Therefore a man shall leave his father and his mother and hold fast to his wife, and the two shall become one flesh' (Matt. 19:5).

Why is this significant? Why does it matter that Jesus is quoting Genesis? For starters, Jesus' use of these verses from Genesis helps us understand how to use the Bible and points us to a framework for understanding God's design for sexuality. Jesus refers to Genesis 1 and 2 because these chapters present God's uncorrupted, undistorted, original design for humanity—before sin entered the world in Genesis 3.

Don't miss this point. Sin corrupts and distorts. We live in a post-Genesis 3 world, which means we suffer from the corruption and distortion of sin. Jesus knows this well. In fact, one of the primary reasons Jesus came to earth was to reverse the curse of sin and to help us overcome sin's effects, one of which is distortion and confusion about marriage and sexuality. To this end, Jesus points us back to God's original design for us: 'from the beginning it was not so.'

In other words, Jesus wants His hearers to return to Eden to consider God's original design for human relationships. As we wrestle with questions related to human sexuality, following Jesus' lead and studying the passages He cites is a great place to start.

How was sin distorting the Pharisees' approach to Jesus?

How does sin affect our ability to understand God's Word? To ask questions? To obey God's will?

By connecting Genesis 2:24 with Genesis 1:27, Jesus teaches not only the *what* of God's design but also the *why*. We could probably come up with thousands of variations on how God could have made human relationships to be. For example, instead of creating Adam and Eve, God could have made one person who could reproduce asexually, like some plants and animals do. Or, God could have created all of the people who would ever exist at the same time, with no reproduction necessary! But by putting Genesis 2:24 next to Genesis 1:27 and connecting them with the word 'therefore,' Jesus is telling us that there is a *purpose* behind why God created humans the way He did.

> **PRINCIPLE:** *When reading and interpreting the Bible, context is key. We must give due regard to a passage's immediate literary, historical, and canonical contexts. This means that we should read the text in light of its immediate context, its historical situation, and within the greater unfolding story of Scripture, which is as one, unified book made up of many divinely inspired books.*

Consider Genesis 2:24's surrounding context. Genesis 2:4–23 provides a detailed account of the creation of the first man and woman, the first human couple. This passage begins with God fashioning Adam from the dust of the ground and breathing life into him. Then, God charges Adam to keep and work the ground and name the animals (vv. 15, 19–20). Next, God creates Eve, the first woman, as Adam's helpmate and presents her to him. Significantly, after God creates Eve and brings her to Adam, the biblical author interjects his own inspired interpretation of the meaning of this first marriage. This marriage will be the paradigm for all other marriages that follow.

> Therefore a man shall leave his father and his mother and
> hold fast to his wife, and the two shall become one flesh.
> **GENESIS 2:24**

The 'therefore' in verse 24 is explaining what came before in Genesis 2:4–23. It is for this reason that God made Adam and Eve and brought them together the way He did. Again, God could have made Adam and Eve differently. He could have created them simultaneously or with identical features. But He made them the way He did for a reason, and that reason is explained in Genesis 2:24.

Understanding the context of Genesis 2:24 infuses Jesus' words in Matthew 19 with added significance. When Jesus says, 'from the beginning it was not so,' and quotes the most important and recognized verse related to God's design for marriage, He is laying out a principle: God has created the world and humanity with a specific design. Thus, whenever we think about marriage, gender, and human sexuality, we ought to filter it through the lens of God's creation design as revealed in Genesis 1 and 2.

> **PRINCIPLE:** *God created the world with a specific design and purpose. God made us male and female for a purpose.*

Have you ever wondered why God created the world the way He did? What other purposes can you see in God's created order?

Think of some similarities and differences between males and females. If these similarities and differences are original and intentional in God's design, what is the implication of Jesus' teaching in Matthew 19? What conclusions can we start to draw about the similarities and differences between male and female purpose?

Weekly Reflection

Main Points from Lesson 1:

In our first lesson, we have looked at Matthew 19:3–9 and Jesus' teaching on marriage. Notably, Jesus references Genesis 1 and 2 when explaining God's design and plan for marriage. Thus, as we consider what the Bible teaches about marriage, gender, and human sexuality, it is wise to start where Jesus (and Paul after Him) starts. It is also important from the outset of our study to ensure we are wisely handling God's Word and interpreting it faithfully. Consider these main points from our lesson and discuss the application questions with your group.

1. When reading and interpreting the Bible, remember that Scripture helps us interpret Scripture.
2. When it comes to reading and interpreting the Bible, context is key—that includes a passage's immediate literary, historical, and canonical contexts.
3. God created the world with a specific design and purpose. God made us male and female for a purpose.

In this lesson, we considered how to interpret the Bible. How can we make sure that we are faithfully interpreting God's Word? Why is it important to ensure that we are not imposing our own ideas or presuppositions onto the text when we read and study the Bible?

Our first lesson in this study is titled 'Creation's Warrant.' Why do we need to know God's original design for marriage and human sexuality? How are Genesis 1 and 2 critical for understanding God's design?

What are you hoping to learn from the rest of our study on marriage, gender, and human sexuality?

This Week's Memory Verse

He answered, 'Have you not read that he who created them from the beginning made them male and female, and said, "Therefore a man shall leave his father and his mother and hold fast to his wife, and the two shall become one flesh?"'
MATTHEW 19:4-5

Conversation Guide Session 1

As Christians, we believe the Bible has all the answers to life's big questions. When it comes to questions related to marriage and human sexuality, do you look to the Bible for answers? Do you know where to look to learn about God's plan for marriage and sexuality?

The world offers limitless answers to questions on marriage and sexuality. This reality can be disorienting and confusing. Who is right? Is there even such a thing as right? The Bible teaches us that God's ways are true and that we can come to Him to learn the truth: 'Teach me your way, O Lord, that I may walk in your truth; unite my heart to fear your name' (Ps. 86:11). Not only this, but God has given us His Word so that we can understand the world and His ways. This is very important: we have the Bible so that we can understand it, and the Bible assumes that it is understandable. Listen to these words from Psalm 119: 'Your word is a lamp to my feet and a light to my path' (Ps. 119:105). Additionally, 'The unfolding of your words gives light; it imparts understanding to the simple' (119:130). This means we can understand what the Bible teaches about marriage and sexuality.

The Bible's vision for marriage and sexuality begins with God's creation of humanity as male and female in Genesis 1 and 2. God's creation of one man, Adam, and one woman, Eve, not only sets the trajectory for the rest of the human race but also acts as a kind of plumb line, or standard, for modeling and assessing human sexuality.

How does Jesus answer the Pharisees' question in Matthew 19? Specifically, how does He use Old Testament Scripture to point to something even deeper than what they asked Him about?

Jesus answers the Pharisees' question by pointing them to Scripture, specifically the chapters in the Bible that describe God's pre-Fall creation. Here we find an important hermeneutical principle: we should interpret Scripture with Scripture. This principle is sometimes called the 'rule of faith' or 'analogy of faith.' It is a commitment to understanding verses and chapters of the Bible in light of the whole Bible, which helps us interpret those passages that are more difficult to understand with passages that are easier to understand. Every word of the Bible is inspired by God (2 Tim. 3:16), which means we cannot simply ignore or discard those verses that we do not understand or do not like. But because every word is inspired, we are confident that pursuing the whole Bible's teaching on a particular subject will lead us to a unified picture, not a contradiction.

Jesus pointed the Pharisees to the deeper truth that not everything in the Bible is recorded to be imitated or to reveal God's moral will. There are things in the Bible that are contrary to God's will, like when the Israelites made a golden calf to worship at Sinai, or when Solomon took many wives. Jesus said that God permitted divorce, but this was not part of God's original design for marriage and family. We must look elsewhere for God's design: Genesis 1 and 2.

What is Jesus referring to when He says, 'but from the beginning it was not so'? How does Jesus' use of Scripture help us understand God's original plan for the created order?

When Jesus says, 'from the beginning it was not so,' He is pointing us back to God's original design in creation. The 'beginning'—God's creation before sin entered the world—shows us God's design and purpose, especially for marriage and family. Jesus has a concept of the way things are (after sin entered the world and hardened our hearts) and the way things were or should be (when God created the world without sin). This concept gives us an aim, a *telos* (τέλος)—a Greek word that means 'end' or 'fulfillment'—to shoot for, and what we should be aiming for is the absence of sin, toward God's creation in the beginning. It's like Jesus is presenting Genesis 1 and 2 as a kind of North Star for our moral compass when it comes to marriage and sexuality. The farther away we get from this picture, the farther away we get from God's will for us as male and female.

How was sin distorting the Pharisees' approach to Jesus?

Sin was causing the Pharisees to approach Jesus with an air of skepticism. They attempted to trap Him in a contradiction or trap Him in opposing God's Word. The trap didn't work as they intended; instead, it closed on them. But sin was also distorting the Pharisees' concept of marriage. For one, they were asking Jesus about an expansive and erroneous interpretation of God's Word on divorce—the passage they ask Jesus about in Deuteronomy does not say that a man can divorce his wife for any reason. Secondly, they did not understand the difference between regulating a sinful practice and endorsing sin. Jesus makes it clear in His answer that God's original design for marriage is that it is to be lifelong and committed.

How does sin affect our ability to understand God's Word? To ask questions? To obey God's will?

Sin can blind us to the truth by either keeping us from it altogether or causing us to ignore or deny the truth when confronted by it. The sin of pride keeps us from seeking God (Ps. 10:4), and it can cause us to dismiss biblical truth as outmoded, outdated, or irrelevant. This denial of God's truth leads to futile thinking and foolish hearts that are darkened to the light of God's Word (Rom. 1:21).

Have you ever wondered why God created the world the way He did? What other purposes can you see in God's created order?

The Bible points to the way God created the world to teach us about the will of God for the world. We see this in 1 Timothy 2:12–14 and 1 Corinthians 11:3–10, where Paul points to God's order in creating Adam first and then Eve, and Eve for Adam, to inform the order of the home and church.

God's process in creating the world also seems to progress in glory from day one to day six, culminating in the creation of humanity as male and female in God's image, informing humanity's dignity, purpose, and worth. God's creation of the world in six days and rest on the seventh inform our week — this point is explicitly mentioned in Exodus 20:11. God's creation work in Genesis 1 and 2 not only gives us a kind of blueprint that God followed when creating the world but also a blueprint for our lives that we can follow.

> **Think of some similarities and differences between males and females. If these similarities and differences are original and intentional in God's design, what is the implication of Jesus' teaching in Matthew 19? What conclusions can we start to draw about the similarities and differences between male and female purpose?**

Men and women, males and females, are different! And they are different in complementary ways: men have external genitalia, women internal. Women can bear children (if reproductively healthy), men cannot. Men can sire children, women cannot. Men give either an X or Y gene in procreation, women can only give an X. The way we are designed, which is by God's design, should inform our purpose and function.

Week 2

CREATION'S ORDER

SEX, GENDER, NATURE, AND MARRIAGE

Individual Experience

Read this section before your group meets

As we saw in the first chapter of our study, the Bible teaches us that God's creation work in Genesis 1 and 2 should inform our understanding of what God made, how He made it, and why He made it to be so. In other words, the creation order gives way to a creation purpose.

God's original design of the world gives us an idea of what God intends for His creation, including His creation of humanity as male and female.

A Christian understanding of human sexuality begins where the Bible begins, in Genesis 1 and 2. These chapters not only explain that God created humanity male and female but also why—and one of the central reasons is marriage.

Human nature comes in two complementary forms. We refer to these forms as the sexes: male and female, man and woman. God created humanity this way with a specific design and function in mind. Even if we didn't have God's special revelation in Scripture, God's design for male and female would still be visible to us. Our very bodies bear witness to God's purpose in making us male and female: it is built into our nature. Without the complementary design and function of male and female, the human race would cease to exist, as we would no longer procreate.

DEFINITION OF NATURE: In this study, the word 'nature' refers to God's original design and purposes in creation. This is the word's traditional sense and the sense we see used in the Bible (e.g., Romans 1:26–27).

God's Word helps us interpret nature according to God's design and purpose. Through God's Word, we learn more about God's design for marriage.

After providing an overview of God's creation of the world, Genesis 1 concludes with the creation of the first human couple. Genesis 1:26–28 explains that God created Adam and Eve in His own image and tasked them with the responsibility to 'be fruitful and multiply and fill the earth and subdue it.' Together, the first human pair reflect God to the rest of creation in a unique way and are responsible for exercising dominion and filling the earth.

Genesis 2 develops the teaching about God's creation of male and female in His image. Although everything was declared 'good' in Genesis 1, God says in Genesis 2:18 that it is not good for Adam to be alone and declares His intention to create a helper fit for Adam. After Adam is unable to find a suitable companion in the process of naming the animals, God causes a deep sleep to fall over the man and creates the first woman out of Adam's own flesh (Gen. 2:21-22). When God presents Eve to Adam, the man proclaims:

'This at last is bone of my bones and flesh of my flesh; she shall
be called Woman, because she was taken out of Man.'
GENESIS 2:23

Immediately after Adam's pronouncement, the author pauses the narrative and provides an editorial note that frames and informs all subsequent biblical reflections on marriage:

Therefore a man shall leave his father and his mother and hold
fast to his wife, and they shall become one flesh. And the man
and his wife were both naked and were not ashamed.
GENESIS 2:24-25

When understood in context, this passage teaches several important truths about human sexuality. Although some are called to a life of singleness—and this is God's good design and plan for these individuals—still, marriage is the norm throughout human history and still today.

God's original design for male and female includes the sexual potential for procreation within marriage. Even if that potential is never realized and marriage or having children is not part of an individual's life experience—and we must acknowledge this is the case for many, even some that desire otherwise—one's bodily constitution is nevertheless the product of male-female union and points toward God's design for marriage.

Genesis 1 and 2 teach us the important truth that we must first understand God's design for marriage in order to understand God's design for human sexuality. We could say the creation order gives us our 'orders.'

What is marriage?

We can define marriage in two ways. First, we can define marriage in terms of the bare minimum requirements that must be in place for a union to be called a marriage. Second, we can define marriage in terms of what God designed marriage to be, even though some of those purposes may be thwarted in a fallen world. For example, while procreation is not necessary for the formation of a bona fide marriage covenant, procreation is nevertheless God's design for marriage. In defining marriage, it is important that we give careful attention to both ways of defining the term.

First, sexual differentiation is part of God's design for marriage. God created two, complementary, biologically (and genetically) sexed individuals, not two androgynous beings. In other words, God built the complementarity of the sexes into the very fabric of creation. God's creation of male and female is not accidental or incidental; it is central to God's design of human beings created in His image. In Genesis 1, the mandate to be 'fruitful and multiply' is given to both the man and the woman; neither could fulfill this charge alone. Thus, what is referred to today as the 'gender binary' is rooted in the order of creation.

Second, marriage is exclusive. The 'one flesh' union between a husband and wife is a bond that joins spouses to each other in a profound way. This new union is a powerful force that needs to be safeguarded. This intimate bond requires exclusive devotion to the marriage partner; union with another violates that bond. For this reason, Scripture treats adultery and other forms of sexual immorality very seriously (e.g., 1 Cor. 6:12-20). Even lustful thoughts directed toward another person who is not one's spouse are a violation of the exclusive devotion and faithfulness that belong in marriage (Matt. 5:28).

Third, marriage is permanent. A man and woman leave their families of origin and unite in a life-long relationship. When questioned about marriage in Matthew 19, Jesus cites Genesis 2:24 and emphasizes the permanence of marriage: 'So they are no longer two but one flesh. What therefore God has joined together, let not man separate' (Matt. 19:6; cf. Mark 10:9).

Finally, marriage is a sacred covenant. Whereas most contracts between adults may be entered and severed at will without severe consequences, a sacred covenant is a permanent agreement established before God. God is personally involved in marriage, which is why it is sacred. Jesus explains this in Matthew 19 by reiterating that God joins couples in marriage. Because of the sacred nature of marriage, a man and woman should enter it reverently, discreetly, advisedly, soberly, and in the fear of God.

As our lesson has shown, the Bible provides God's vision for marriage. Scripture teaches that marriage is exclusive, permanent, and a sacred covenant. Moreover, sexual differentiation is part of God's design for marriage.

What stood out to you about the Bible's definition of marriage?

Which part do you think our culture has an especially hard time understanding?

Life Application

We all encounter rival concepts of God and the world when we interact with people outside of the Christian faith—and sometimes even with people who confess Christ. So, how should we talk about God's original design with them?

We should be willing to be upfront with our own fundamental faith commitments, such as our belief that God created the world and designed it with a purpose. But we can also seek to establish common ground with non-believers by appealing to what theologians have called 'general revelation.'

General revelation is knowledge about God's character and purposes that can be recognized by anyone via natural means (e.g., reason, observing nature), without the help of 'special revelation' (e.g., Scripture, prophets, miracles). The Bible tells us that God's creation testifies about its Designer. Consider Romans 1:20:

> For his invisible attributes, namely, his eternal power and divine
> nature, have been clearly perceived, ever since the creation
> of the world, in the things that have been made.
> **ROMANS 1:20**

And Psalm 19:1-2:

> The heavens declare the glory of God, and the sky above proclaims his handiwork.
> Day to day pours out speech, and night to night reveals knowledge.
> **PSALM 19:1-2**

Evolutionary biologists will occasionally use the language of 'design' or 'purpose' to describe features of the created world, a world that they believe is the result of a cosmic accident. Although evolutionary biologists attribute any apparent 'design' to millions of years of natural selection, they nonetheless recognize a utility or a function to a creature. For example, during his field studies in 1862, Charles Darwin came across an orchid flower from Madagascar that had an extremely long nectar tube. Because he knew how these kinds of flowers were pollinated, he knew there must be a large, moth-like insect with a massive tongue as long as the nectar tube that could pollinate this species. The problem was, no one had ever seen such a creature in Madagascar. But Darwin predicted its existence by his understanding of design and function. It wasn't until 1903, over fifty years later, that this moth was discovered and cataloged, proving Darwin's prediction right. The point of this story is not to prove Darwin right in every respect (we think his theories about macro-evolution are wrong) but to show that an intellectually honest observer of nature and creation will see that there is an underlying design to the world. The incredibly intricate design elements we see play out with respect to male and female across the animal kingdom give us common ground to talk about form and function.

Ultimately, the Bible helps us make total sense of God's creation in general revelation. Still, God's world acts as a kind of tutor in the ways of God and can help us have conversations about the creation order with our neighbors about our Creator God.

Watch

Follow along as you watch the video for Session 2.

This page is provided for you to take notes as you watch the video.

Group Experience

When Jesus is asked a question about sexuality and sin, He directs His listeners back to the first chapters of the Bible in Genesis 1 and 2 to remind them of God's original design for human sexuality. In these two chapters, we saw that God designed male and female sexuality with marriage and procreation in mind.

A proper understanding of marriage grounds sexual morality. God designed our sexuality to have a proper aim: marriage. The implication is that any sexual activity that is not within the bounds of God's design for marriage is sin. In other words, a proper understanding of the design can help us see why going against that design is harmful, or what the Bible calls sinful.

When we understand the creation order and God's design for marriage, we can better understand what the Bible teaches to be disorder, or sin. An analogy would be studying a genuine $100 bill—its characteristics, qualities, and unique attributes—in order to be able to detect counterfeit bills.

What does the creation order tell us about God's desire for humanity?

One way to think about the relationship between the creation order and human sexuality is to consider how and why certain tools are designed the way they are. For instance, you don't use a hammer to paint your room, and you don't use your toothbrush to dig a hole. Technically, you could do these things, but there is an obvious, designed function that you are ignoring when you paint with a hammer or dig with a toothbrush, and there is a much better aim, or telos (purpose, fulfillment), for these tools that you would be ignoring.

Similarly, when we act against our nature, our design, and our purpose given to us by our Maker as male or female, we not only harm ourselves but also disrespect the One who made us.

How does studying nature and the creation order help us better understand and appreciate God's design and purposes for humanity?

Through natural revelation and the fact that God's design is built into our very bodily structures, humanity has been able to approximate the Bible's teaching on human sexuality throughout history and across societies, even while falling far short of it.

Think about it. A simple understanding of marriage and procreation helps us to see that societies will quite literally cease to exist without some form of this institution being preserved. This is why God's design for marriage is not only the bedrock for a right understanding of human sexuality, but it is a bedrock for the family and human society as well.

Should we be surprised to see a biblical understanding of human sexuality and marriage under such attack today?

A right understanding of marriage is important for the church for two indispensable reasons:
1) Marriage is the measure of sexual morality. But there is another, perhaps even more important reason why a right understanding of marriage is so important for the life and health of the church. 2) Marriage is the central picture God gives us to understand the gospel.

Why is it important to ground sexual morality in God's design for marriage?

Marriage is central to the Bible's story. The Bible begins with a marriage between Adam and Eve in the Garden of Eden, with God presiding as officiant and witness, and the Bible ends in the book of Revelation with the marriage supper of the Lamb.

Why do you think marriage is central to the Bible's story?

The Bible teaches that marriage illustrates and reflects the relationship between God and His people. Paul explains this in Ephesians 5:22–33 while giving instructions to Christian husbands and wives. After describing Christ's sacrificial love for His church, Paul addresses husbands in verse 28, saying:

> In the same way husbands should love their wives as their
> own bodies. He who loves his wife loves himself.
> **EPHESIANS 5:28**

Here, Paul charges husbands to imitate Christ by sacrificially loving their wives. Then, in verses 29–30, Paul explains that human marriage is to be patterned after Christ's relationship with the church:

> For no one ever hated his own flesh, but nourishes and cherishes it, just
> as Christ does the church, because we are members of his body.
> **EPHESIANS 5:29-30**

In verse 31, Paul quotes Genesis 2:24, drawing a parallel between the 'one-flesh' union of human marriage and the union of believers to Christ. By making this connection, Paul makes it clear that God intends marriage to point beyond itself to the relationship between Christ and the church. He states this explicitly in verse 32:

> This mystery is profound, and I am saying that it refers to Christ and the church.
> **EPHESIANS 5:32**

In context, the word 'mystery' refers to something previously hidden but now revealed (Eph. 1:9, 3:3; cf. Rom. 16:25; 1 Cor. 2:7, 10). The 'profound mystery' is that God intended marriage to image the gospel and Christ's redemptive love for His bride from the very beginning. To the degree that our marriages are what God intends them to be, they provide a picture (however imperfect) of the union between Christ and the church, which displays God to the watching world.

How does marriage point to Christ and the church?

The connection between marriage and the gospel is why getting the Bible's testimony wrong on human sexuality is a 'gospel issue.' To get this wrong is to get the gospel wrong.

We are going to revisit this text in the coming weeks, but 1 Timothy 1:8–11 is clear that practicing sexual behavior that is contrary to God's law, and teaching others that it is okay to engage in these behaviors, goes against sound doctrine and the gospel itself:

> Now we know that the law is good, if one uses it lawfully, understanding this, that the law is not laid down for the just but for the lawless and disobedient, for the ungodly and sinners, for the unholy and profane, for those who strike their fathers and mothers, for murderers, the sexually immoral, men who practice homosexuality, enslavers, liars, perjurers, and whatever else is contrary to sound doctrine, in accordance with the gospel of the glory of the blessed God with which I have been entrusted.
> **1 TIMOTHY 1:8-11**

If heterosexual, monogamous, lifelong marriage is the picture that images the gospel, when we distort that image by deviating from God's original design, we distort the gospel itself.

Weekly Reflection

Main Points from Lesson 2:

In our second lesson, we looked at Genesis 1 and 2. As we've discussed, these chapters help us understand God's original plan for marriage. Consider these main points from our lesson and discuss the application questions with your group.

1. God's original design of the world gives us an idea of what God intends for His creation, including His creation of humanity as male and female.
2. Genesis 1 and 2 teach us that we must first understand God's design for marriage in order to understand God's design for human sexuality.
3. The Bible teaches that marriage is the lifelong union of one man and one woman. Marriage is exclusive, permanent, and a sacred covenant. Moreover, sexual differentiation is part of God's design for marriage.

If someone at church or a friend asked you to define marriage, how would you respond?

In light of the high view with which the Bible presents marriage, why is sexual sin so serious?

In this lesson, we've said that marriage is the central picture God gives us to understand the gospel. Do you agree? If marriage is this important, why is it crucial that we get it right?

This Week's Memory Verse

And God blessed them. And God said to them, 'Be fruitful and multiply and fill the earth and subdue it, and have dominion over the fish of the sea and over the birds of the heavens and over every living thing that moves on the earth.'

GENESIS 1:28

Conversation Guide Session 2

DEFINITION OF NATURE: In this study, the word 'nature' refers to God's original design and purposes in creation. This is the word's traditional sense and the sense we see used in the Bible (e.g., Romans 1:26–27).

A quick note on our definition of nature: Some other theological definitions of 'nature' differ from the one we are using in this study. Some people use the word 'nature' when talking about our fallen nature. We think it is most helpful to talk about this kind of nature as 'sin nature.' Our sin nature results from our being children of Adam, whose fall into sin affects the whole human race (Rom. 5:12-14; 1 Cor. 15:21–22). This sin nature is referred to in the Bible as 'the flesh' (cf. Rom. 8:13) and the 'old self' (Eph. 4:20–24).

Other ways the word 'nature' is used is related to what comes 'naturally' to a person. Sometimes this use of the concept of nature is used to try and justify homosexual behavior. For example, if someone feels naturally predisposed to be attracted to the same sex, then what is natural for them is to act according to their 'nature.' But this is where our definition of nature comes in, and we are using it in the technical sense of Romans 1:26–27. There Paul writes:

> For this reason God gave them up to dishonorable passions. For their women exchanged natural relations for those that are contrary to nature; and the men likewise gave up natural relations with women and were consumed with passion for one another, men committing shameless acts with men and receiving in themselves the due penalty for their error.
> ROMANS 1:26-27

What Paul calls contrary to nature is not contrary to their desires; it is contrary to God's original design. This is why understanding God's original creation, or nature, is important. Because we want to lean into God's design, not away from it. And when we have desires or inclinations that go against nature or the way God designed the world to be, we cannot simply cite our own 'natural' impulses as justification. This would be to side with our sin nature over God's design in nature.

What does the creation order tell us about God's desire for humanity?

The creation order reveals God's purpose for His creation. God created men and women, male and female, as complements of one another. In every detail of the design, down to our very reproductive organs, male and female have complementary features that fit with one another. This creational design points to a creational purpose: marriage and companionship between male and female, husband and wife. That there are two and only two sexes teaches us that marriage is to be between two people; that the two are complementary and not interchangeable teaches us that marriage is to be between a man and a woman, and that a man cannot marry another man, or a woman another woman. That a male-female sexual union has the potential to procreate offspring teaches us that marriage is the foundation for the family and, in turn, society.

How does studying nature and the creation order help us better understand and appreciate God's design and purposes for humanity?

Studying the creation order attunes us not only to how God created the world but also the purposes He has for creating the way He did. We live in a post-Genesis 3 world, where sin has ravaged God's original design, even to the point of compromising our own thinking—what theologians call the noetic effects of the Fall. The result is that our perceptions and inclinations can be distorted, and we should assume that there are some things about our world today that are not original to God's design. What is original to God's design? Humanity created male and female for marriage, procreation, dominion, stewardship, etc. We see this when we go back to 'the beginning' (cf. Matt. 19:1–9).

Should we be surprised to see a biblical understanding of human sexuality and marriage under such attack today?

Human sexuality and marriage are all original and natural to God's creation in the beginning. Therefore, the constant attack on sexuality and marriage that we are witnessing today is an attack on God's plan and will for humanity. Moreover, God created us male and female to bear His image apart from all creation. The attempt to redefine sexuality and marriage proceeds on the faulty assumption that God is not deeply invested in these elements that are native to the creation order. To attack these is to attack the very fabric of the natural order, creation. The enemy wants nothing more than to steal, kill, and destroy (John 10:10), and what better target is there than the very institution of marriage and family, the incubator of humanity and God's image-bearers, and structural support of this institution in sexuality.

What is more, where marriage is at stake, the gospel is at stake because God chose marriage to be the picture that would communicate Christ's love for His church (Eph. 5:31–32). We shouldn't be surprised when those who are opposed to God are opposed to God's prized institutions.

Why is it important to ground sexual morality in God's design for marriage?

God's design for marriage is the purpose of our sexuality. When we pursue sexuality outside of this aim and fulfillment, we are going against God's design. This is why sexual desires and acts outside of the covenant bond of marriage are forbidden in Christian morality, not only because God says they are sinful but also because He knows what is best for His creatures and does not want harm to come to them. Acting in ways that contradict the original design is like filling up your car's gas tank with tomato juice and expecting it to run just fine because you know it gives you energy when you drink it. Cars are not designed to run on tomato juice but gasoline—just like we aren't designed to drink gasoline for energy. Ignoring God's original design for sex and marriage is not only sinful, but it is bad for you. And God loves you enough to tell you so.

Why do you think marriage is central to the Bible's story?

Marriage is central to the Bible's story because, from the very beginning, God had a plan to redeem humanity by sending His Son to die on the cross and rise again from the dead in order to ratify a permanent, unbreakable covenant with His people. The Bible also teaches us that God is love (1 John 4:8), which means that God in His nature is relational—not only Triune as Father, Son, and Holy Spirit but also overflowing with love for His creation.

In this way, marriage is designed to teach us about God's love for his people in the gospel.

How does marriage point to Christ and the church?

Paul explains in Ephesians 5:22–32 how marriage points to Christ and the church:

> Wives, submit to your own husbands, as to the Lord. For the husband is the head of the wife even as Christ is the head of the church, his body, and is himself its Savior. Now as the church submits to Christ, so also wives should submit in everything to their husbands.

> Husbands, love your wives, as Christ loved the church and gave himself up for her, that he might sanctify her, having cleansed her by the washing of water with the word, so that he might present the church to himself in splendor, without spot or wrinkle or any such thing, that she might be holy and without blemish. In the same way husbands should love their wives as their own bodies. He who loves his wife loves himself. For no one ever hated his own flesh, but nourishes and cherishes it, just as Christ does the church, because we are members of his body. 'Therefore a man shall leave his father and mother and hold fast to his wife, and the two shall become one flesh.' This mystery is profound, and I am saying that it refers to Christ and the church.

Christ's marriage to His church is consummated at the marriage supper of the Lamb, which we read about in Revelation 19:6–9, when God's people are united to God for eternity:

Then I heard what seemed to be the voice of a great multitude, like the roar
of many waters and like the sound of mighty peals of thunder, crying out,
'Hallelujah!
For the Lord our God
the Almighty reigns.
Let us rejoice and exult
and give him the glory,
for the marriage of the Lamb has come,
and his Bride has made herself ready;
it was granted her to clothe herself
with fine linen, bright and pure'—
for the fine linen is the righteous deeds of the saints.
And the angel said to me, 'Write this: Blessed are those who are invited to the
marriage supper of the Lamb.' And he said to me, 'These are the true words of God.'

Week 3

SIN'S DISORDER

EXCHANGING THE TRUTH OF GOD FOR A LIE

Individual Experience

Read this section before your group meets

God's special and distinct design of male and female has implications for our sexual lives. Our bodies are organized for reproduction either in a male way (fathering) or a female way (mothering). The Bible's teaching testifies concretely to what we can see with our eyes in nature. The Bible also fleshes out the nature of the marriage covenant and what is required of us. Thus, nature and Scripture reveal that the one-flesh union of male and female in marriage is God's design for our sexuality.

Nevertheless, by nature, sinners rebel against God's beautiful design for his male and female image-bearers. That rebellion takes many forms. Some rebel against the notion that sex should be restricted to the marriage covenant. Others wish to redefine the marriage covenant so that it is no longer permanent (i.e., no-fault divorce). Still others wish to redefine the marriage covenant so that it might include multiple sexual partners (i.e., adultery, polyamory, polygamy) or even same-sex sexual partners (i.e., homosexuality). All of these are distortions of God's original design for our sexuality, and thus all of them constitute sinful rebellion against our Creator.

It is clear now that the sexual revolution of the 1960s and 1970s has brought a sustained assault on the Christian foundations of sexual morality. As old norms have collapsed, Christians in the West face new challenges to what God has revealed about sexuality and gender. Many are kicking against the goads of God's design, and many in our culture now embrace sexual practices that were once considered taboo even among secular people. This change has happened very rapidly, and perhaps on no issue has this change been more evident than it has been with homosexuality.

Not only has the secular culture grown in its acceptance of homosexuality, but also some professed Christians have spread false teaching claiming that the Bible itself permits homosexuality.

What are we to make of these arguments? Does the Bible teach that homosexuality is sinful and contrary to God's design for sexuality? Or are others correct when they say loving and committed same-sex relationships are consistent with the Bible's teaching? These are serious questions that merit our attention.

In this lesson, we will take a closer look at what the Bible teaches on homosexuality.

Leviticus 18:22 and 20:13

Perhaps the most concise prohibition on homosexuality in the Old Testament is found in Leviticus. The book of Leviticus contains two explicit proscriptions concerning homosexuality.

They read:

'You shall not lie with a male as with a woman; it is an abomination.'
LEVITICUS 18:22

'If a man lies with a male as with a woman, both of them have committed an abomination; they shall surely be put to death; their blood is upon them.'
LEVITICUS 20:13

These verses call a sexual relationship between two men an abomination. The word used in both verses is the Hebrew word *toebah*, which is translated as 'detestable' (NIV, NLT, CSB) or 'abomination' (ESV, NASB, KJV). In context, both verses appear within lists prohibiting a wide range of sexually immoral behaviors. This is important because some interpreters have claimed that the passages only condemn homosexual activity in the context of pagan worship or temple prostitution. However, the verses surrounding Leviticus 18:22 and 20:13 place broad prohibitions on other forms of sexual sin, such as incest (18:6-18), bestiality (18:23), adultery (18:20, 20:10), or forcing a daughter into prostitution (19:29).

The prohibitions in Leviticus forbid even general, consensual homosexual activity. The second passage (Lev. 20:13) makes this evident when it says that both men have committed an abomination and shall be punished. Thus, the command is straightforward: men are prohibited from having sex with men.

Romans 1:18-32

Romans 1:24-27 contains perhaps the most important teaching in the Bible on homosexuality:

Therefore God gave them up in the lusts of their hearts to impurity, to the dishonoring of their bodies among themselves, because they exchanged the truth about God for a lie and worshiped and served the creature rather than the Creator, who is blessed forever! Amen. For this reason God gave them up to dishonorable passions. For their women exchanged natural relations for those that are contrary to nature; and the men likewise gave up natural relations with women and were consumed with passion for one another, men committing shameless acts with men and receiving in themselves the due penalty for their error.
ROMANS 1:24-27

A few details of this passage are important for our study. The first is Paul's use of the creation narrative to frame his discussion of humanity's rebellion against God. In addition to allusions to the creation account of Genesis 1 and 2, Paul's choice of language in Romans 1:26-27 underscores the connection to Genesis 1. Paul uses the less common terms *thēlys* (female) and *arsēn* (male) to emphasize the sexual distinctiveness of male and female. For Paul, the corruption of sexuality and humanity's rejection of male-female complementarity are indicative of a departure from God's purposes in creation.

Second, the 'exchange' language in this passage emphasizes humanity's rejection of God and the created order. Paul gives three examples of how what has been known about God has been exchanged for something else. The intentional repetition of 'exchange' draws attention to the undeniable link between the rebellion and its grave consequences.

Third, while describing the sinful 'exchanges' men and women have made, Paul introduces the term *para physin* in verse 26, meaning 'against nature.' Greco-Roman and Jewish writers from the first century used *para physin* in reference to same-sex activity and juxtaposed it with *kata physin* ('according to nature') as a way of distinguishing between heterosexual and homosexual behavior. The text indicates that all same-sex relations were against God's design and intention for human sexuality and a violation of the created order. Sexuality exists to draw men and women together in marriage; homosexual relations upend this design.

Fourth, homosexuality is a consequence of humanity suppressing God's truth and refusing to honor Him, and its consequences are a sign of God's judgment. Paul's analysis leads to a sobering conclusion: flagrant, high-handed, and unrepentant sin—including homosexual activity—is evidence of God's present-day wrath. The flouting of sexual distinctions and homosexual activity are indicators of this judgment.

Finally, Romans 1:18-32 sets up Paul's condemnation of all human sin. Paul's Jewish readers would have readily agreed with his assessment of homosexuality. But in Romans 2:1, Paul turns the tables on these would-be-judges who were happy to condemn the Gentiles. He writes, 'Therefore you have no excuse, O man, every one of you who judges. For in passing judgment on another you condemn yourself, because you, the judge, practice the very same things.' God condemns hypocrisy in the same passage that He condemns sexual sin. Everyone stands in desperate need of God's grace.

1 Corinthians 6:9 and 1 Timothy 1:10

The New Testament contains two additional passages that address homosexuality. Both appear in 'vice lists.' In context, they read:

> Or do you not know that the unrighteous will not inherit the kingdom of God? Do not be deceived: neither the sexually immoral, nor idolaters, nor adulterers, nor men who practice homosexuality, nor thieves, nor the greedy, nor drunkards, nor revilers, nor swindlers will inherit the kingdom of God.
> **1 CORINTHIANS 6:9-10**

> The law is not laid down for the just but for the lawless and disobedient, for the ungodly and sinners, for the unholy and profane, for those who strike their fathers and mothers, for murderers, the sexually immoral, men who practice homosexuality, enslavers, liars, perjurers, and whatever else is contrary to sound doctrine.
> **1 TIMOTHY 1:9-10**

These verses are significant for understanding the Bible's teaching on homosexuality.

First, in 1 Corinthians 6, Paul lists different kinds of people who will be excluded from the kingdom of God unless they repent. In the list, Paul includes four references to sexual sin, including two that mention homosexual behavior. The relevant terms are *malakoi* ('soft ones,' 'effeminate') and *arsenokoitai* ('a man who beds a man'). English translators render the two terms in various ways. Some translations combine the terms, whereas others interpret the words separately.

Consider a few examples:

- ESV: 'men who practice homosexuality'
- NASB: 'effeminate' and 'homosexuals'
- KJV: 'effeminate' and 'abusers of themselves with mankind'
- NLT: 'male prostitutes' and '[those who] practice homosexuality'
- NIV (1984): 'male prostitutes' and 'homosexual offenders'
- NIV (2011): 'men who have sex with men'

Malakoi is an adjective meaning 'soft.' When referring to things, *malakoi* describes something that yields to the touch. It can also describe someone or something that is 'effeminate.' In this verse, it refers to men playing an effeminate role in male homosexual encounters. Thus, it describes the passive partner in same-sex immorality.

Some interpreters suggest that the term *arsenokoitai*, when paired with *malakoi*, refers specifically to some kind of exploitative same-sex relationship—either a man with a boy or perhaps a man with a male prostitute. On this basis they falsely claim that this verse does not condemn all homosexual unions but only those that are exploitative. On this reading, the verse doesn't have anything negative to say about committed same-sex unions. It is a clever interpretation designed to convince Bible readers that the Bible actually allows for committed gay relationships.

The problem with this interpretation is that it fails to reckon with Paul's usage of the term. *Arsenokoitai* appears nowhere else in Greek literature until Paul uses the term here. That suggests that Paul coined this term in this very verse. It is a compound word formed by combining *arsēn* ('male') and *koitēs* ('bed'), terms found in the Greek version of Leviticus 18:22 and 20:13. When put together, the new compound refers to a man bedding another male. This is important because Paul identifies homosexual behavior as a sin, and he does so on the basis of Leviticus 18:22 and 20:13. Those verses in Leviticus don't merely condemn exploitative same-sex unions but all same-sex unions.

By using *malakoi* and *arsenokoitai* together, Paul includes both active and passive homosexual partners within his list of unrepentant sinners who will not inherit the kingdom of God.

Finally, in 1 Timothy 1, Paul includes *arsenokoitai* (translated by the ESV as 'men who practice homosexuality') on a list of sins that do not conform to 'sound doctrine' (v. 10). The term means the same thing in 1 Timothy 1:10 that it means in 1 Corinthians 6:9. God's law exposes this sin, and believers are exhorted not to participate in any activity that discredits the gospel or dishonors God (v. 11). Christians should repent of sin and pursue a life that is consistent with their new identity in Christ. Once again, Paul presumes the Old Testament's prohibition on homosexual relations.

Life Application

It can often seem like Bible-believing Christians are standing alone in discussions about sexuality. Professing Christians in theologically liberal denominations amplify this sense of aloneness when they claim that the Bible supports same-sex relations and homosexuality is not sinful.

Yet the perspective presented in this lesson is not a minority opinion or the view of an isolated denomination or sect. Indeed, a brief survey of church history reveals that the church has been clear and consistent on human sexuality since the first century. It is quite significant that despite varying circumstances, pressures, and disagreement on other significant theological issues, Roman Catholics, Protestants, and Orthodox Christians have spoken with one voice in consistently affirming God's design and plan for marriage as laid out in Genesis 1 and 2.

For example, one of the earliest works in Christian apologetics, *The Epistle to Diognetus*, summarizes Christian sexual ethics by saying, 'They marry, as do all [others]; they beget children; but they do not destroy their offspring. They have a common table, but not a common bed.' Early Christians distinguished themselves from the surrounding culture by maintaining a high view of life and marriage and rejecting sexual promiscuity.

As early as the first and second centuries, Christian literature listed sodomy among sins that must be avoided. For example, the *Didache* (AD 50-120) reads: '[T]hou shalt not commit sodomy; thou shalt not commit fornication.' *The Epistle of Barnabas* (written between AD 70-132) also includes a reference to homosexual activity among its prohibited list of behaviors.

Early Christian leaders were direct in their condemnation of homosexuality. For example, in his commentary on Leviticus 18, Eusebius of Caesarea (263-339) says the passage forbids 'all unlawful marriage, and all unseemly practice, and the union of women with women and men with men.' Likewise, Basil the Great (330-379) wrote, 'He who is guilty of unseemliness with males will be under discipline for the same time as adulterers.' In a homily on Romans 1:26-27, John Chrysostom (c.347-407) also disapproved of homosexuality. Using a variety of descriptions, he says same-sex relations are 'shameful deeds,' 'an insult to nature itself,' 'contrary to nature,' 'lawless love,' a 'grievous evil,' and 'unseemly.'

In short, Christian teaching on homosexuality remained unbroken into the twentieth century. In 1951, Karl Barth reflected the prevailing view of Christian theologians when he said, 'the decisive word of Christian ethics must consist of a warning against entering upon the whole way of life which can only end in the tragedy of concrete homosexuality.'

This remained the view of every Christian denomination until the latter half of the twentieth century. Only then, at the height of the sexual revolution, did many mainline Protestant denominations such as the Episcopal Church, Presbyterian Church (USA), and Evangelical Lutheran Church in America change their view on homosexuality.

It is worth noting that the churches that changed their view on the nature of marriage over the last few decades were the same churches that, since the 1920s, had increasingly embraced theological liberalism. The correlation between rejecting the Bible as God's infallible and authoritative Word (which also means rejecting the Bible's accounts of miracles, the deity of Christ, and the historical reliability of the Bible) and the acceptance of homosexuality is striking, given that denominations that continued to believe in the trustworthiness and reliability of the Bible remained committed to Christianity's historic teaching on sexuality.

Watch

Follow along as you watch the video for Session 3.

This page is provided for you to take notes as you watch the video.

Group Experience

In the 'Individual Experience,' we looked at the Bible's teaching on homosexuality by taking a closer look at Leviticus 18:22 and 20:13, Romans 1:18-32, 1 Corinthians 6:9, and 1 Timothy 1:10. Along with Genesis 19:4-14, these passages present the Bible's teaching on homosexuality and show how departures from God's design for sexuality are not only sinful but harmful.

We'll begin our time as a group by considering a few discussion questions that prompt reflection about the material we've studied so far.

Based on our study, what does the Bible teach about homosexuality? How would you respond to someone that says that the Bible doesn't talk about homosexuality?

Some have argued that verses like Leviticus 18:22 and 20:13 are not binding on Christians because they are part of the old covenant. Why are these verses relevant for how Christians should understand the Bible's position on homosexuality?

Why is the Bible's teaching on homosexuality important for Christians?

As we've seen, the Bible is clear in its moral evaluation of homosexuality. It may not be popular to talk about sexual ethics, but it is important to know that God's Word addresses these topics. Moreover, Christians have been consistent in their understanding of the Bible's teaching on these questions for millennia. In fact, as we have seen in our 'Life Application' section for this week, Christians, since the first century, have taught that sexuality is the basis of the desire for male and female to be united in a one-flesh union called marriage. The Bible teaches that sexual desire draws people to marriage, not merely to sex (see Genesis 1 and 2). Thus, a Christian understanding of marriage must govern a proper understanding of sexuality.

Considering the Bible's teaching on marriage and sexuality brings us to our current cultural moment. Seemingly overnight, the moral framework underlying Western culture has been upended, and centuries of norms concerning the family, marriage, and sexuality have been overturned. How did this happen? How did behavior and lifestyles condemned nearly universally as immoral a generation ago become accepted and now celebrated in such a short amount of time?

What are some of the developments of the twentieth century that contributed to the revolution in morality we've witnessed over the last few decades?

Thus far, we've reflected on several biblical texts that indicate the Bible's moral appraisal of homosexuality. However, there is another passage that deserves our attention: Genesis 19:4-14. The term 'sodomy' has become synonymous with homosexual immorality because of the terrifying display of God's judgment on Sodom and Gomorrah in this text. However, some revisionists have argued that Sodom's sin had nothing to do with consensual, committed same-sex relationships. Rather, they point to Ezekiel 16:49 and contend that greed, corruption, and inhospitality are to blame for the cities' destruction. The passage reads:

> Behold, this was the guilt of your sister Sodom: she and her daughters had arrogance, abundant food, and careless ease, but she did not help the poor and needy. Thus they were haughty and committed abominations before me. Therefore I removed them when I saw it.
> **EZEKIEL 16:49-50**

Those who affirm homosexuality often use Ezekiel 16:49 to make the case that Sodom's offense in Genesis 19 had nothing to do with homosexuality but with social injustice. They observe that Ezekiel's description of Sodom in verse 49 focuses on hard-heartedness toward the 'poor and needy' without saying anything at all about the attempted homosexual rape that is famously recorded in Genesis 19.

The problem with this interpretation is not that it is wrong about social injustice recorded in verse 49. The problem is that it stops at verse 49 without adequately accounting for the sin listed in verse 50. Verse 50 confirms that in addition to social injustice, Sodom also had 'pride' and 'committed abominations.' The Hebrew word for abomination is *toebah*, which Ezekiel's readers would have immediately recognized as a call-back to the holiness code in Leviticus 18-20, where the term *toebah* describes God's detestation of sexual sin—in particular the sin of homosexuality.

> You shall not lie with a male as with a woman; it is an abomination (*toebah*).
> **LEVITICUS 18:22**

> If a man lies with a male as with a woman, both of them have committed an abomination (*toebah*).
> **LEVITICUS 20:13**

When Ezekiel says that Sodom had 'pride' and 'committed abominations,' he is explicitly linking Sodom's sin to the homosexual acts that God condemns in Leviticus 18:22 and 20:13.

It is worth noting how Ezekiel lists 'pride' right before Sodom's sexual 'abominations.' This is no accident. Pride refers to Sodom's boastful and self-regarding arrogance. As the Bible teaches elsewhere, whatever is in the heart will eventually spill out into action. The Lord Jesus Himself confirms that this is particularly true of sexual sin (Matthew 5:28). The people of Sodom had arrogance in their hearts, and that pride turned out to be the wellspring of sin, including their abominable sexual immorality.

And perhaps that is the real lesson to be learned during the annual observance of 'Pride' month in June. Pride is not something to celebrate or flaunt. It is a grave sin in need of repentance before a holy God. Eventually, those who approve of homosexuality will find out that even their affirmation is a grave sin. For judgment falls not only on those who commit abominable sins but also on those who 'give approval to those who practice them' (Rom. 1:32).

Which interpretation of Genesis 19:4-14—the traditional or affirming—is more faithful to what the passage teaches? How do we respond to those who argue that Sodom's sin was a failure to show hospitality and that homosexuality is not a major reason for God's judgment?

Of course, the Bible's teaching on homosexuality is contested. Increasingly, opposition comes from all corners of society, including the media, entertainment, and business communities. Antagonism toward orthodox Christian beliefs on these issues has become commonplace, and even some who regularly attend Bible-believing churches are struggling to accept what the Bible teaches on marriage and homosexuality. This reality was underscored by a 2020 study by George Barna that revealed that 34 percent of American evangelicals reject the definition of marriage as a relationship between one man and one woman for life.

But despite widespread rejection of biblical sexual ethics, Christians must hold firm to the Bible's teaching on sexuality, which includes understanding homosexuality as a departure from God's original design. This is non-negotiable. The Bible does not allow for relationships, lifestyles, or activities that transgress God's divinely established boundaries.

While our culture sees these teachings as outdated and even subversive to happiness in the modern world, the Bible is nevertheless clear in its presentation of God's plan for sexuality. As a matter of Christian faithfulness and witness, Christians must believe, teach, and live out these teachings.

Finally, as we conclude this week's study, we need to consider those in our circles who struggle with homosexuality. While the final lesson in our study will discuss how the gospel reframes our identity, it's important to recognize that readers who experience same-sex attraction may feel discouraged after reading this week's lesson which covers the teaching of the Bible and church history on this topic. It is, therefore, important to remember the full context of the verses we have considered. We must remember that the Bible's teaching on sexuality is something we all need to hear, but it is not all we need to hear. Scripture teaches that homosexual practice is contrary to God's design for sexuality, but this is not the Bible's central focus.

Homosexuality, along with fornication, adultery, lust, greed, and a catalog of other sins, are all signs of living in a fallen world where even our deepest thoughts and desires are confused. Christians ought to understand this dynamic better than anyone and be the first to respond to hurting people with grace and mercy.

In Ephesians 4:15, Paul tells his readers to 'speak the truth in love.' How do we speak the truth in love when it comes to contested issues such as same-sex marriage and homosexuality?

It is true that Christians have not always been good at speaking 'the truth in love' with their friends and neighbors who identify as LGBTQ. In fact, some in the LGBTQ community have had negative experiences with the church and, as a result, believe Christians are mean, judgmental, and hateful. Admittedly, some Christians have been unkind, unloving, and even hateful toward people who identify as LGBTQ. Where this is true, we should be honest about our own shortcomings. Scripture says Christians should be known by their love (John 13:35). If we have failed to properly show love to our neighbors who identify as LGBTQ, we ought to repent and seek forgiveness. As those filled with God's Spirit, followers of Jesus should be marked by their joy, patience, kindness, and gentleness (Gal. 5:22-23), not anger, vitriol, or lack of compassion.

The church ought to be the place where all people can hear the gospel, find people willing to share their burdens and struggles, and learn what it means to find their identity in Christ. When individual Christians or the church-at-large fails to treat their LGBTQ-identifying neighbors with true dignity or neglect to offer them the full gospel, they are not only failing LGBTQ-identifying people; they are failing to live out the second-greatest commandment (Matt. 22:39) and Great Commission (Matt. 28:16- 20). The church should stand as a pinnacle of clarity and hope, affirming God's design for humanity amidst the confusion of our various experiences and proclaiming God's faithfulness to rescue us from our sin.

Weekly Reflection

Main Points from Lesson 3:

In 1 Corinthians 6, Paul says that the unrighteous will not inherit the kingdom of God. But immediately after condemning those living in habitual, unrepentant sin, he reminds his readers of the gospel and their identity in Christ. Some of his readers once practiced these things— 'such were some of you.' But not anymore. Paul can now say to these former habitual sinners, including those who practiced homosexuality, that they were 'washed...sanctified...[and] justified in the name of the Lord Jesus Christ and by the Spirit of our God.' When someone comes to Christ, there is a transformation in identity. That was true in first century Corinth and is still true today. Consider these main points from our lesson and discuss the application questions with your group.

1. The Bible teaches that homosexuality is a sin and contrary to God's design for sexuality.
2. Despite recent suggestions to the contrary, Christians have affirmed the Bible's teaching on sexual ethics for 2,000 years.
3. The gospel offers the hope of redemption, healing, and reconciliation to anyone struggling with sexual sin.

Is the Bible's teaching on homosexuality important? Why is it a matter of Christian faithfulness to affirm what the Bible teaches on this topic?

Considering passages like 1 Corinthians 6:11, how does the gospel transform our identity?

Jude 3 says we must 'contend for the faith that was once for all delivered to the saints.' Why is it important for Christians to contend for the whole counsel of God's Word, including Christian sexual ethics, which are under constant assault?

This Week's Memory Verse

And such were some of you. But you were washed, you were sanctified, you were justified in the name of the Lord Jesus Christ and by the Spirit of our God.

1 CORINTHIANS 6:11

Conversation Guide Session 3

Based on our study, what does the Bible teach about homosexuality? How would you respond to someone that says that Bible doesn't talk about homosexuality?

There are only six explicit references to homosexuality in the Bible, but every single one of those references condemns it as sin: Genesis 19:4-14, Leviticus 18:22 and 20:13, Romans 1:18-32, 1 Corinthians 6:9, and 1 Timothy 1:10. This week's lesson provides exegesis on these passages. For a more in-depth study of these passages, see Robert Gagnon's 'The Bible and Homosexual Practice.' For a succinct treatment of these passages, see 'Biblical Principles for Human Sexuality,' available for free at FRC.org/HumanSexuality.

Some have argued that verses like Leviticus 18:22 and 20:13 are not binding on Christians because they are part of the old covenant. Why are these verses relevant for how Christians should understand the Bible's position on homosexuality?

In response to the plain meaning of the text, some have argued that these verses are not binding because they are part of the old covenant. The thinking runs along these lines: since Christians live under the new covenant that was inaugurated by the death and resurrection of Christ, these prohibitions no longer apply. However, these arguments are misleading for two reasons.

First, Paul's word on homosexuality is taken directly from Leviticus 18 and 20. In this way, the apostle clearly communicates the abiding relevance of Leviticus 18:22 and 20:13 for believers in the new covenant. Moreover, the prohibitions on homosexuality are found within a literary unit that includes laws that are still relevant for Christians. These include bans on incest, adultery, child sacrifice, lying, slander, and taking God's name in vain. Also, the second-greatest commandment— to love your neighbor as yourself— appears in this section (Lev. 19:18). Surely, Christians are still bound to these laws even if they are not bound to the Mosaic law.

Second, the New Testament authors base their sexual ethic on the Law of Moses and make that ethic binding on all believers. If one of the laws in Leviticus is no longer binding, there should be a New Testament passage that makes this clear. For example, in the New Testament, God explicitly repealed Old Testament laws prohibiting certain foods (see Acts 10:9-23). Likewise, laws about sacrifices were repealed, i.e., fulfilled by Christ (see Heb 10:11-14). In short, a principle of biblical interpretation is that if the New Testament repeats an Old Testament provision, it is reinforced. In the case of homosexuality, the New Testament reinforces the clear prohibition of the Old Testament.

Why is the Bible's teaching on the topic of homosexuality (and any other topic it addresses) important for Christians?

Second Timothy 3:16 teaches that 'All Scripture is breathed out by God and profitable for teaching, for reproof, for correction, and for training in righteousness, that the man of God may be complete, equipped for every good work.' Christians believe the Bible is authoritative, inerrant, and infallible. As such, Christians ought to submit to the Bible in all areas of their lives. If the Bible teaches that a certain behavior or action is contrary to God's design for human flourishing, it is our responsibility to order our lives according to His plan, not ours. In fact, Scripture teaches us not to be conformed to this world but to be 'transformed by the renewal' of our minds (Rom. 12:1).

What are some of the developments of the twentieth century that contributed to the revolution in morality we've witnessed over the last few decades?

At least four cultural developments paved the way for the moral revolution. First, the rise of urbanization offered new opportunities for anonymity. In 1800, 7 percent of the world's population lived in cities. Today, 55 percent of the world's population lives in dense population centers. By 2050, it is projected that this number will rise to 68 percent. One of the social effects of the rise of dense population centers is the erosion of community-based accountability that often exists in rural and less-populated areas. In other words, the rise of cities helped remove a societal check against premarital and extramarital liaisons by lowering the chance of discovery and exposure.

Second, advances in contraceptive technology—such as 'the Pill'—separated sex from potential pregnancy in many people's minds. Albert Mohler notes, 'Once the Pill arrived, with all its promises of reproductive control, the biological check on sexual immorality that had shaped human existence from Adam and Eve forward was removed almost instantaneously.' (The quote appears in Mohler, *We cannot Be Silent*, p. 11.) Whereas before the potential consequence of conceiving a child served as a natural deterrent from premarital or extramarital sex, the Pill allowed for seemingly consequence-free sexual activity.

Third, laws that restricted certain sexual behaviors and conduct were replaced or overturned. For example, access to birth control expanded dramatically following two U.S. Supreme Court cases, *Griswold v. Connecticut* (1965) and *Eisenstadt v. Baird* (1972). In *Griswold,* the Court over-turned a state law that prevented married women from accessing birth control. In *Eisenstadt*, the Court extended contraceptive access to unmarried couples. Today, legal precedent has established a broad view of individual liberty regarding personal and intimate decisions. Recent evidence for this includes the Supreme Court's decision in 2015 to legalize same-sex marriage in *Obergefell v. Hodges*. Significantly, the majority in *Obergefell* based its decision on a very expansive view of liberty, arguing that the U.S. Constitution promises liberty to the extent that people may 'define and express their identity.' The culture and mainstream legal philosophy have propagated a new autonomous being who alone may shape his or her identity and sexual behavior.

Finally, a fourth development contributing to the moral revolution is Christianity's loss of cultural influence. According to Pew Research, in 2019, 65 percent of American adults described themselves as Christian—down 12 percentage points from 2009. In the same time period, the percentage of Americans who identify with no religion rose 26 percent—up from 17 percent in 2009. The rise in religious 'nones' is most pronounced among the younger generations. These changes in America's religious demographics mean that fewer people understand or hold Christian convictions, including those relating to sexual morality.

Additional trends—such as cohabitation, absentee fathers, no-fault divorce, pornography, and abortion—have also contributed to weakening the family and society's moral malaise.

Which interpretation of Genesis 19:4-14—the traditional or revisionist—is more faithful to what the passage teaches? How do we respond to those who argue that Sodom's sin was a failure to show hospitality and that homosexuality is not a major reason for God's judgment?

Recent revisionist interpreters have argued that the focus on same-sex behavior in Genesis 19 is not a faithful reading of the text. They argue that sexual violence or gang rape appear to be the main issue and that other parts of the Bible (including Ezekiel 16:49) reinforce the idea that Sodom's sin was sexual violence or inhospitality. Ezekiel 16:49 says, 'This was the guilt of your sister Sodom: she and her daughters had pride, excess of food, and prosperous ease, but did not aid the poor and needy.' While homosexuality is not mentioned in this verse, a closer look at Ezekiel 16 shows that sexual sin, particularly homosexuality, is still in view.

Ezekiel continues his discussion of Sodom's guilt in the next verse: 'They were haughty and did an abomination before me' (v. 50). The Hebrew word *toebah*, translated by the ESV, NASB, and KJV as 'abomination' is rendered 'detestable' by the NIV, CSB, and NLT. *Toebah* is the same word used in Leviticus to refer to homosexual acts. Thus, while the term is used elsewhere in the Old Testament to refer to a wide array of sins, homosexuality cannot be ruled out. In the New Testament, two passages provide further clarity that sexual immorality is at the root of Sodom's sin. In 2 Peter 2:6, Peter explains that Sodom and Gomorrah stand as an 'example of what is going to happen to the ungodly.' He says that Lot was rescued after being 'greatly distressed by the sensual conduct of the wicked' (v. 7). Moreover, in verse 10, Peter makes a broader point about the unrighteous, noting that those who 'indulge in the lust of defiling passion' will not escape judgment. In context, Peter's mention of Sodom in a passage about the sensuality of false teachers underscores the sexual nature of Sodom's crime.

Jude 7 is the second New Testament passage that mentions Sodom and Gomorrah, and it connects the cities' overthrow with an unnatural sexual immorality. Jude mentions the apostate inhabitants of Sodom and Gomorrah and their severe punishment. He describes the inhabitants of these cities as those who 'indulged in sexual immorality and pursued unnatural desire' (v. 7). 'Unnatural desire' is translated in the NASB as 'strange flesh.' The Greek phrase *sarkos heteras* means 'different or another flesh.' Jude is clear that Sodom's sin was more than attempted rape or a desire to have sex with angelic beings. Rather, the very nature of the desire of the city's men was disordered.

In Ephesians 4:15, Paul tells his readers to 'speak the truth in love.' How do we speak the truth in love when it comes to hotly debated issues such as same-sex marriage and homosexuality?

Christians are commanded to be truth-tellers. This principle should apply to every aspect of a believer's life. This is underscored in Ephesians 4:15, where Paul uses the verb *alētheuō* which means 'speaking the truth.' In context, it appears Paul is concerned that the Ephesian Christians are speaking the truth about the gospel. The only other time the verb appears in the New Testament is in Galatians 4:16, where the gospel is clearly in view: 'Have I then become your enemy by telling you the truth?' Thus, while Paul is encouraging his readers to speak the truth about the gospel, mentions of 'doctrine,' 'spiritual maturity,' 'the unity of the faith,' and 'deceitful schemes' in the immediate context show that Paul's command to speak the truth is not limited to speaking truthfully about the gospel. Rather, Christians are to speak and embody God's truth in their daily lives as part of their pursuit of unity in the church. Moreover, pursuing truth must be characterized by a love that is willing to sacrifice and serve others; a combative or irritable spirit is out of place for Christians seeking to build up the body in love.

When it comes to speaking the truth in love about same-sex marriage and homosexuality, Christians must speak clearly about God's revealed truth on these matters. The Bible's moral appraisal of homosexuality is unambiguous (Gen. 19:4-14; Lev. 18:22, 20:13; Rom. 1:18-32; 1 Cor. 6:9; 1 Tim. 1:10). Christians cannot muddle what the Bible teaches. But the tone and posture of one's heart are also important. Christians must be characterized by compassion, grace, and kindness. A Christian's love toward another person should never be in doubt (Mark 12:31). A mark of Christian maturity is the ability to speak forthrightly yet winsomely (especially on divisive topics). In one's articulation and presentation of doctrine, zeal for truth and love for a fellow image-bearer is crucial for faithful gospel witness.

Week 4

TEMPTATION, DESIRE, AND ORIENTATION

Individual Experience

Read this section before your group meets

Much of the material in the following section follows closely the presentation in Denny Burk and Heath Lambert, Transforming Homosexuality *(P&R, 2015).*

The Anatomy of Desire

In the last chapter, we established the Bible's basic teaching about sexual morality. Any sexual activity outside the covenant of marriage is sinful. This would, of course, prohibit any kind of non-marital cohabitation, adultery, homosexual relationships, and countless other perversions outside of the covenanted union of one man and one woman in marriage. Therefore, our study thus far has given us biblical clarity about prohibited sexual behaviors. But what does the Bible say about our sexual feelings? Is God only concerned about our sexual behaviors, or is He interested in sanctifying our sexual desires as well?

In Matthew 5:27-28, Jesus answers these questions by explaining the real meaning of the seventh and tenth commandments (Exod. 20:14, 17). He says, 'You have heard that it was said, "You shall not commit adultery"; but I say to you, that everyone who looks on a woman to desire her sexually has already committed adultery with her in his heart' (our translation). Jesus instructs His disciples that it's not merely certain sexual behaviors that are sinful but also certain kinds of sexual desires.

This raises a number of questions for us.

How do I know the difference between a sinful sexual desire and a non-sinful one?

What about temptation? Does this mean that my experience of sexual temptation is sinful?

How does all of this apply to people who experience sexual desires for persons of the same sex? Are they sinning in their desires even if they never act on those desires?

Discerning Sinful Sexual Desire

How do we know the difference between a sinful sexual desire and a non-sinful one? Some people think that the difference lies in whether one chooses to feel the desire in question. For example, if a man chooses to feel sexual lust for another man's wife, that would be sinful. According to this view, a man's spontaneous and unchosen feelings of sexual attraction for another man's wife would not be sinful. Other people suggest that perhaps the difference resides in the intensity of the desire. According to this view, intense sexual desires for another man's wife are prohibited, but passing sexual interest is no harm or sin at all.

Is the difference in either the chosenness or intensity of the sexual desire? Will a wife be comforted by her husband's assurances that he only feels a little bit of sexual desire for her best friend? No, the low intensity of her husband's adulterous desire will be little comfort, for any amount of sexual desire for another woman is unfaithfulness. Will she be comforted to learn that his adulterous sexual desires spring up spontaneously with no conscious decision on his part to feel those desires? No, that knowledge only makes the treachery more deeply entrenched in his character. It is neither the intensity nor the chosenness of his illicit desire that makes it sinful. So then, what distinguishes a sinful sexual desire from a righteous sexual desire?

Jesus teaches that the object of the desire determines the moral character of the desire. If one desires sin, then the desire itself is sinful, regardless of the desire's intensity or chosenness. Notice that Jesus' teaching in Matthew 5:27–28 is merely His exposition of the seventh and tenth commandments. The seventh commandment prohibits adultery, while the tenth commandment prohibits the desire for adultery (Exod. 20:14, 17). The tenth commandment makes clear that it's not merely the doing of sin that is sinful but also the desiring for sin. Jesus, the master teacher, makes clear what the Law of Moses taught all along. Our sexual desires matter to God.

If the root of sexual sin is in the heart, what does that tell us about repentance? If sexual sin is first of all a matter of the heart, then why does Jesus tell disciples to cut off their hand or gouge out their eye in order to avoid sexual sin?

Discerning Sinful Sexual Temptation

What about temptation? Does this mean that my experience of sexual temptation is sinful? Since sinless Jesus was tempted in the same way I am (Heb. 4:15), doesn't that mean that temptation is never by itself sinful?

To answer these questions, we must come to terms with what the Bible says about temptation. All temptation has two components to it—a trial and an enticement. The trial of temptation consists of some hardship, suffering, or deprivation. The enticement of temptation consists in the allure to relieve that hardship, suffering, or deprivation through sinful means. When the devil tempted Jesus in the wilderness, both components of temptation were present. The trial is Jesus' hunger and thirst after forty days of fasting. The enticement is the devil's appeal to Jesus to relieve this suffering by obeying the devil's command, 'command these stones to become loaves of bread' (Matt. 4:3). There was no sin on Jesus' part in undergoing temptation by the devil. Jesus was tempted in every way that we are, yet He was and is always without sin (Heb. 4:15). He never faltered.

Nevertheless, we must acknowledge that sometimes our experience of temptation is quite different from Jesus'. And that difference is in the last phrase of Hebrews 4:15. Jesus was tempted as we are, yet He was always 'without sin.' We must be careful not to confuse our sinful experience of temptation and Jesus' sinless experience of temptation. Jesus had no sin nature. Every other person who has ever lived does have a sin nature.

That means that sometimes we are tempted by our own sinful desires. As James writes:

> But each person is tempted when he is lured and enticed by
> his own desire. Then desire when it has conceived gives birth
> to sin, and sin when it is fully grown brings forth death.
> **JAMES 1:14-15**

As the sinless Son of God, Jesus never had a sinful desire. Thus, He was never tempted by His own sinful desire, for He never had such desire for evil. The same is not the case with us. When we are enticed by our own sinful desires to do evil, the temptation itself is sinful.

Is temptation sinful? Not necessarily, but it can be. Jesus' temptations were wholly external to His nature and desires. Thus, they were not sinful. When we experience temptation from the outside, like Jesus did, the temptation involves no sin on our part. But when our temptations emerge from our own sinful nature and desire, the temptation itself is sinful and is an occasion for repentance.

What is the main difference between Jesus's experience of temptation and our own experience of the same? Have you ever experienced a temptation that felt like illicit desire emerging from your own heart?

In this lesson, we are thinking about desire and temptation.

Based on what we've considered, how would you explain the difference between a sinful sexual desire and a non-sinful one?

Life Application

In his commentary on James 1, Sam Allberry explains the relationship between temptation to sin and desire to sin this way:

> The uncomfortable truth is this: the evil desire tugging away at us is our own. We can't blame any of the things around us. It is not the fault of our parents, our peers, our circumstances, our genes or our God... My circumstances may be the occasion for my sin, but they are not the cause of it.
>
> No, our own desires are the cause of temptation. The desire to sin that wells up within us comes from our own hearts. Temptation would not be tempting if I were pure and not evil. This is reinforced by what James tells us about how temptation works...
>
> James is showing us something deeply profound about our human nature, for we are both agent and victim of our desires. The desires are our own, from our own hearts—yet it is us that they entice and attack. Within each of us there is this deep tension. We really are our own worst enemies (pp. 34-35).

This view of human sinfulness, which is the way the Bible talks about our relationship with sin, has a lot of explanatory power for how we experience sinfulness in the world. We are sinners by nature and by choice. We inherit Adam's corruption and have a sinful nature and desires before we ever choose to do a sinful deed. That is what James is talking about. Our fallen desires produce our fallen choices, and both are indeed sinful.

With this understanding, we should be both less surprised and more troubled by our own sinfulness and the sinfulness of those around us. We want to sin because we are predisposed to it and because our fallen human nature enjoys sin. But that is where the gospel is so freeing: it explains our predicament and doesn't see it as insurmountable—just the opposite. This is the very power Jesus came to free us from, the power of sin and death (Rom. 8:2).

Watch

Follow along as you watch the video for Session 4.

This page is provided for you to take notes as you watch the video.

Group Experience

Discerning Sinful Sexual 'Orientations'

If the Bible indeed teaches what we saw in the last section—that the sinfulness of a desire is determined by its object, and temptations that arise from our own hearts are sins—what about same-sex desire and temptation?

Do these principles apply to people who experience sexual desires for persons of the same sex? Are they sinning in their desires even if they never act on those desires? Is a homosexual orientation or identity itself sinful?

Now, at the outset, it is important for us to state that we are not singling out same-sex desire for particular condemnation. The Bible's teaching on temptation and desire cuts against both heterosexual and homosexual sin. When Jesus talked about sexual desire, it was heterosexual sin — 'looks on a woman to desire her sexually (our translation)'—that He was talking about. And desire for something that God forbids is sin—and that would include any sexual desire that is aimed outside the marriage covenant.

But we live in a day and age where the Bible's teaching against homosexuality is under fire, especially when we talk about 'orientation.'

Some writers have argued that the concept of sexual orientation is a modern one and that the biblical writers therefore don't really address the possibility that someone might have a homosexual orientation. Some writers even suggest that because the biblical writers didn't know about homosexual orientation, their various condemnations of homosexual behavior are not really addressing people who have a homosexual orientation. For example, they would say that the condemnations of homosexual behavior in Romans 1 are aimed at people with a heterosexual orientation acting against their orientation. But the apostle Paul did not have in view people with a homosexual orientation living in committed same-sex relationships. Thus, the biblical prohibitions on homosexual behavior do not apply to people with a homosexual orientation.

The problems with this reasoning are manifold. One of the main problems is the claim that the Bible knows nothing of the concept of 'orientation.' This claim fails to reckon with what modern people mean when they speak of orientation. The American Psychological Association defines orientation this way:

> Sexual orientation refers to an enduring pattern of emotional, romantic and/or sexual attractions to men, women or both sexes. Sexual orientation also refers to a person's sense of identity based on those attractions, related behaviors and membership in a community of others who share those attractions (Source: www.apa.org).

Notice that sexual orientation refers to the direction of one's sexual attractions or desires. If one experiences an enduring sexual desire for persons of the same sex, that person is said to possess a 'homosexual orientation.'

But as we have seen above, the Bible speaks explicitly to our sexual desires—heterosexual, homosexual, or otherwise. And the Bible says that if the object of our sexual desire is sinful, then the sexual desire itself is sinful. This truth is not mitigated by the fact that some illicit desires may be 'enduring.' Orientation is simply the enduring experience of a certain species of sex desire, and the Bible speaks to that reality very clearly. Therefore, to say that the Bible doesn't know or speak about the concept of orientation is false.

To the degree that one builds a self-identity on the foundation of illicit sexual desire, that identity, too, would be a sinful identity at odds with one's identity in Christ.

Would it be right for a Christian to embrace a homosexual identity so long as they reject homosexual behavior?

Instead, there is a better way to think about our identity, and that is to build one's self-identity on creational order. We will talk more about this in Week 7.

But in the meantime, we would do well to close this week with a positive vision of desire. After all, desire and affection are designed by God as well, and we should seek to be people whose desires are conformed to God's law. It is fleshly desire we are called to mortify—and fleshly desire is any desire that is opposed to God's will and purposes in creation and redemption.

Take a moment to read Galatians 5:16-24.

But I say, walk by the Spirit, and you will not gratify the desires of the flesh. For the desires of the flesh are against the Spirit, and the desires of the Spirit are against the flesh, for these are opposed to each other, to keep you from doing the things you want to do. But if you are led by the Spirit, you are not under the law. Now the works of the flesh are evident: sexual immorality, impurity, sensuality, idolatry, sorcery, enmity, strife, jealousy, fits of anger, rivalries, dissensions, divisions, envy, drunkenness, orgies, and things like these. I warn you, as I warned you before, that those who do such things will not inherit the kingdom of God. But the fruit of the Spirit is love, joy, peace, patience, kindness, goodness, faithfulness, gentleness, self-control; against such things there is no law. And those who belong to Christ Jesus have crucified the flesh with its passions and desires.

This passage teaches us that those who have the Spirit have two desires at war within themselves: the desires of the flesh and the desires of the Spirit. Notice carefully that desires of the flesh are related to 'sexual immorality, impurity, sensuality.' The word for 'sexual immorality' is a word that refers to any sexual deviance that does not accord with God's original design, whether heterosexual or homosexual.

But this passage teaches us that there are desires that accord with God's Spirit, and these will produce the fruit of the Spirit. In order to pursue these, we must crucify the flesh with its sinful passions and desires.

In other words, the call to follow Christ is certainly a call to self-denial—Jesus couldn't have been clearer in Matthew 16:24 when He said:

> If anyone would come after me, let him deny himself
> and take up his cross and follow me.
> **MATTHEW 16:24**

But it is more than that, too. It is a call to a fulfillment of true and wholesome desire. This is what Jesus meant when He continues in Matthew 16:25:

> For whoever would save his life will lose it, but whoever
> loses his life for my sake will find it.
> **MATTHEW 16:25**

Do you see the paradox? Through self-denial, through 'losing' one's life, we actually 'find' our true lives, our true selves.

This is what Psalm 145:18–19 says:

> The Lord is near to all who call on him,
> to all who call on him in truth.
> He fulfills the desire of those who fear him;
> he also hears their cry and saves them.
> **PSALM 145:18-19**

When we desire God and His will and deny our fleshly desires that are not in line with His Word, we experience true, everlasting life.

We do so by following and trusting the One who perfectly desired and fulfilled God's law, the man Christ Jesus, whose Spirit gives us new hearts and affections.

Weekly Reflection

Main Points from Lesson 4:

In our fourth lesson, we have addressed the nature of desire, temptation, and orientation as they pertain to sexual sin. Various passages reveal that sexual immorality includes not only the action of a sin but also the desire to sin. This has significant implications for how we should fight temptation and how we should think about the concept of sexual orientation.

Consider these main points from our lesson and discuss the application questions with your group.

1. Jesus taught that the object of a desire determines its moral character. This means that not only the action of a sin, but also the desire to sin in a specific way, is sinful.
2. Temptation is not inherently sinful; however, it can be sinful when it emerges from our own desire for sin.
3. In order to pursue desires that accord with God's Spirit, we must crucify the flesh with its passions and desires.

We learned that if one desires sin, the desire itself is sinful. How does God transform our desires when we submit to Him?

The Bible teaches that Jesus was tempted in every way, yet without sin. How was Jesus's experience with temptation different from our own?

How would you respond to someone who identifies as having a homosexual orientation and believes they are avoiding sin by not acting on their desires?

This Week's Memory Verse

But the fruit of the Spirit is love, joy, peace, patience, kindness, goodness, faithfulness, gentleness, self-control; against such things there is no law. And those who belong to Christ Jesus have crucified the flesh with its passions and desires.

GALATIANS 5:22-24

Conversation Guide Session 4

How do I know the difference between a sinful sexual desire and a non-sinful one?

The sinfulness of a desire is determined by its object, whether the particular object is forbidden by God in a particular situation or not. Some objects of desire are always forbidden—murder, adultery, etc.—while some objects of desire may be forbidden in some contexts and not others—sex, food, comfort, etc.

What about temptation? Does this mean that my experience of sexual temptation is sinful?

Temptation to sin can come from one of two sources: external or internal. External sources of temptation are not sinful unless they arouse desire for what is being tempted. Internal sources of temptation are sinful because they arise from our own hearts. This is what James 1 teaches us. Jesus was tempted externally yet never sinned. We are tempted both externally and internally, and both situations give us an opportunity to turn from temptation and choose God's will for our lives.

No matter what a person's sexual feelings are (homosexual, heterosexual, or otherwise), no person will be delivered from sexual temptations completely in this life. Our response to sexual temptation requires constant vigilance. We must flee from temptation so as not to give in to it (2 Tim. 2:22). If the temptation is arising from our own sinful desires, we must repent of those desires by setting our mind, heart, and affections on things that are true, good, and praiseworthy (Phil. 4:8; Col. 3:2). It's a daily battle for every Christian.

How does all of this apply to people who experience sexual desires for persons of the same sex? Are they sinning in their desires even if they never act on those desires?

Homosexual desire is sinful because its object is something God forbids—sexual intimacy with someone of the same sex—and it arises from a sinful heart. Even if these desires are never acted on, they are still sinful. That said, repentance concerns specific sin and desire. This is why speaking of someone as a 'homosexual' or 'heterosexual' is not technically biblical. Someone either has homosexual or heterosexual desires or commits homosexual or heterosexual acts, and their sinfulness is determined by what God allows or forbids. God calls homosexuality a sin, which means any desire for homosexual immorality is sin that should be repented of.

If the root of sexual sin is in the heart, what does that tell us about repentance? If sexual sin is first of all a matter of the heart, then why did Jesus tell the disciples to cut off their hand or gouge out their eye in order to avoid sexual sin?

Sin ultimately is a heart issue. This includes sexual sin. It is possible to reform the outward man while still harboring sin in the heart. This is why Jesus called the Pharisees 'whitewashed tombs' and 'hypocrites.' Often, we use the word hypocrite to describe someone who believes something they don't live out. But Jesus used the word hypocrite to describe those who acted out something they didn't really believe in their hearts. Listen to His words in Matthew 23:27-28: 'Woe to you, teachers of the law and Pharisees, you hypocrites! You are like whitewashed tombs, which look beautiful on the outside but on the inside are full of the bones of the dead and everything unclean. In the same way, on the outside you appear to people as righteous but on the inside you are full of hypocrisy and wickedness (NIV).'

What is the main difference between Jesus's experience of temptation and our own experience of the same? Have you ever experienced a temptation that felt like illicit desire emerging from your own heart?

Jesus experienced temptation externally, but His pure and sinless heart never was a safe harbor for sinful desires or acts. This is what we mean when we say Jesus is sinless. When we face temptation, however, our sinful hearts not only often harbor such temptations, but they can be the origin of such temptations. Jesus' experience of temptation does not make Him less able to relate to us in our sin. Just the opposite. The author of Hebrews says Jesus is able to sympathize with us in our weakness because He 'has been tempted as we are, yet without sin' (Heb. 4:15). Jesus experienced the full force of temptation and yet never sinned. We do not feel the full brunt of temptation in the same way because we often succumb to temptation in our sinful hearts. Jesus never succumbed to sin, which means He knows temptation better than we do and thus can help us in our temptation.

When we experience temptation emerging from our hearts, we should immediately turn from such temptation—repent of it—and use the opportunity to praise God for His grace in allowing us to turn from it.

Based on what we've considered, how would you explain the difference between a sinful sexual desire and a non-sinful one?

A sinful sexual desire is desire for any sexual intimacy that God has forbidden either through His design and command, like forbidding homosexual acts, or through subjective situations, like desiring sexual intimacy with someone who is not your spouse. A righteous sexual desire is in line with and aimed at what God has permitted and designed, namely within the covenant of marriage.

Do these principles apply to people who experience sexual desires for persons of the same sex? Are they sinning in their desires even if they never act on those desires? Is a homosexual orientation or identity itself sinful?

Sexual desire for a person of the same sex is sinful because God has forbidden same-sex intimacy, which goes against His good design for male and female. Even if someone who experiences same-sex attraction never acts on his or her desires, the desire is still sinful. When people talk about homosexual orientation, this is often what they mean: a person who experiences a pattern of homosexual desire. The homosexual pattern is sinful because each homosexual desire is sinful, which means that a homosexual orientation is sinful.

Would it be right for a Christian to embrace a homosexual identity so long as they reject homosexual behavior?

No. A Christian who embraces a homosexual identity as constitutive to who they are is not living according to what the Bible teaches in 1 Corinthians 6:9–11:

> 'Or do you not know that the unrighteous will not inherit the kingdom of God? Do not be deceived: neither the sexually immoral, nor idolaters, nor adulterers, nor men who practice homosexuality, nor thieves, nor the greedy, nor drunkards, nor revilers, nor swindlers will inherit the kingdom of God. And such were some of you. But you were washed, you were sanctified, you were justified in the name of the Lord Jesus Christ and by the Spirit of our God.'
> **1 CORINTHIANS 6:9-11**

Christians are not defined by their sin but by the finished work of Christ. Such 'were some of you'—but no longer. Christians are not 'men who practice homosexuality' or those defined by their desire to practice homosexuality. Instead, Christians are washed, sanctified, and justified in the name of the Lord Jesus Christ.

Week 5

TRANSGENDERISM

Individual Experience

Read this section before your group meets

In his book *When Harry Became Sally*, Ryan Anderson observes that 'America is in the midst of what has been called a "transgender moment." Not long ago, most Americans had never heard of transgender identity, but within the space of a year it became a cause claiming the mantle of civil rights' (p. 1). Anderson is no doubt correct in his observation. There can be no question that a revolution has swept through not only America but also much of the Western world on the concept of 'gender identity.'[1]

Throughout human history, most people have assumed a natural connection between one's biological sex and one's self-understanding as male or female. In recent decades, however, that natural connection has been severed in the minds of many people in the West. Gender is now widely construed as a social construct that is not dictated by biological sex. There are many reasons for this shift in thinking. Tracing them all would go beyond the scope of this study. Our aim in this chapter is simply to understand what God's Word reveals to us about this new ideology and how we can faithfully follow Christ in a cultural context that is radically opposed to what God's Word says about sex and gender.

Before proceeding with our discussion, we need to clarify some terminology. According to the American Psychological Association, *gender identity* 'refers to a person's internal sense of being male, female or something else' (ww.apa.org). *Transgender* is a catch-all term that refers to the many ways that people might perceive their gender identity to be out of sync with their biological sex.

Until relatively recently, *The Diagnostic and Statistical Manual of Mental Disorders* (DSM), had classified the transgender experience as 'Gender Identity Disorder.' But in 2013, the DSM-5 removed this experience from its list of disorders and replaced it with the term gender dysphoria. It did this in part to remove the stigma from the transgender experience—so that transgender people wouldn't have to say they had a psychological disorder. Instead of pathologizing this experience, the DSM-5 simply focuses on relieving the 'dysphoria' (or mental distress) that some people experience as a result of their perceived gender identity being out of sync with their biological sex.

Simply discussing the meaning of these terms reveals that we are dealing with radical changes in society's understanding of sex and gender—changes that stand in direct contradiction to Scripture. It is, therefore, of utmost importance that Jesus' disciples learn how to distinguish truth from error when it comes to sex and gender.

---

1. I [Denny Burk] have delivered the material from this chapter in numerous conferences and churches over the years. The same material is reflected in Denny Burk, 'Transgenderism and Three Biblical Axioms,' in *God's Glory Revealed in Christ: Essays on Biblical Theology in Honor of Thomas R. Schreiner*, ed. Denny Burk, James M. Hamilton Jr., and Brian Vickers (Nashville, TN: B&H, 2019), 211–25.

The Distinction between Male and Female is Biological

The Genesis creation narrative spells out the fundamental difference between male and female according to God's original design. As Genesis 1:26-27 explains:

> Then God said, 'Let us make man in our image, after our likeness.
> And let them have dominion over the fish of the sea and over the
> birds of the heavens and over the livestock and over all the earth
> and over every creeping thing that creeps on the earth.'
>
> So God created man in his own image,
> in the image of God he created him;
> male and female he created them.
> **GENESIS 1:26-27**

Notice in verse 26 that the accent is on what the man and the woman have in common. They are both created in God's image, and they are both given the responsibility to rule over God's good creation. They are to rule on God's behalf over the world that God has made.

But in verse 27, the accent is on difference. 'So God created man in his own image, in the image of God he created him; male and female he created them.' These two divine image-bearers come in two distinct genres—male and female. And it is precisely here that biblical revelation stands in direct contrast to the aims and purposes of the transgender moment we find ourselves in.

What do we mean by this? It's not that there is a real controversy today (at least at the popular level) about there being a difference between male and female. The controversy is about how to define the difference.

What makes male and female different? Is it a biological thing, a self-concept, or something else altogether?

Some have suggested that brain structures and function are what determine one's sex, not one's reproductive structures. Thus, one's fallen self-understanding would determine so-called gender identity, but reproductive anatomy would not. But that suggestion does not square with the creation narrative from Genesis. Genesis 1:28 says:

> And God blessed them. And God said to them, 'Be fruitful
> and multiply and fill the earth and subdue it.'
> **GENESIS 1:28**

God's words to the male and female, 'Be fruitful and multiply,' are what have become known as the creation mandate. This mandate prescribes procreation within the covenant of marriage. In that context, the terms 'male' and 'female' cannot be referring to brain structures because human beings don't procreate with their brains. In context, male and female are distinguished by their respective reproductive systems. Male and female, therefore, refer to the differing ways that human bodies are organized for sexual reproduction. We now know that this binary organization involves the male alone producing small gametes (sperm) and the female alone producing large gametes (eggs).

The implication of this teaching is clear. If a person's body says 'male' while the brain says 'female,' the brain is wrong. In a fallen world where sin corrupts our mind as well as our bodies, what we think about ourselves can be mistaken. And that is certainly the case with transgender experience. The distinction between male and female is first of all biological, and the biological distinction in view has to do with a body's organization for reproduction—quite apart from any consideration of brain structures.

If this is true, then there are massive implications for how you are supposed to minister the gospel to people dealing with gender-confused feelings. It means that you can tell them on the authority of God's Word that their body isn't lying to them. A person's maleness or femaleness isn't socially constructed or self-constructed but God-constructed. Sex is not something that is assigned at birth. It is something that is revealed by God in His special distinct design of male and female bodies.

Gender Fluidity?

Without a biological basis for understanding sex and gender, there are no guardrails left to determine a definition of either. If biology isn't determinative, anything goes. The biological basis for a binary understanding of gender and sex is that normal genomic chromosomes come in two forms: XX or XY. Under natural development, every cell in a female's body is XX and every cell in a male's body is XY. (We are going to address exceptions to this rule in the next chapter.) But if you throw this biological basis out the window, what now determines one's sex or gender? What determines even the options available?

This is why we have seen the transgender conversation move so rapidly from individuals claiming to transition from male to female, or female to male, to now individuals claiming to be beyond the sexual binary entirely, as they identify as non-binary or gender fluid. The possibilities really become endless, only limited by the imagination.

Do you see how untethering gender from one's sex—or one's nature—can be so destructive?

In this week's lesson, we are trying to think biblically about a topic that is very controversial in our culture today. Consider and reflect on these two questions:

Have you found transgender ideology a difficult topic to discuss at church? If so, what makes this topic challenging to talk about?

How is untethering gender from one's sex destructive?

Life Application

How do we refer to people who have adopted a transgender identity? Many LGBTQ advocates argue that we must refer to those who identify as transgender by their chosen name and pronouns instead of their given name and pronouns that match their biological sex. Should Christians go along with these new speech codes?

Here are some guidelines for you to consider as you think through this thorny issue.

1. Speak the Truth in Love

Disciples of Jesus must always tell the truth (Eph. 4:15). We are not allowed to speak in ways that are fundamentally dishonest and that undermine the truth of God's Word about how He made us. Transgender ideology is fundamentally a revolt against God's truth. It encourages people—sometimes very disturbed and hurting people—to deny who God made them to be, trapping them in a way of thinking that is harmful to them and that alienates them from God's truth. We do not serve them or love them well by speaking as if transgender fictions are true.

We are called not to participate in the unfruitful deeds of darkness, but instead to 'expose them' (Eph. 5:11). That means we must always 'speak the truth in love' (Eph. 4:15). We must realize that real love always 'rejoices with the truth' (1 Cor. 13:6).

Just as the doctor does his patient no favors by speaking in ways that conceal an unpleasant diagnosis, we do our neighbors and loved ones no favors by speaking in ways that conceal the truth of God. The proverb says, 'Faithful are the wounds of a friend, But deceitful are the kisses of an enemy' (Prov. 27:6 NASB). That means that an enemy will tell you what you want to hear, but a real friend will tell you what you need to hear. So, loving our neighbor means telling them the truth, even when that truth brings an unpleasant confrontation.

The practical upshot of this principle means that I must never encourage or accommodate transgender fictions with my words. In fact, I have an obligation to expose them (Eph. 5:11). For that reason, I must never refer to a biological male with female pronouns or to a biological female with male pronouns. I must speak truthfully. And that includes the choice of pronouns that I use.

The use of a legal name may present a special case. Truth-telling with respect to pronouns is one thing, but truth-telling with a person's proper name may be another. What if you don't know a person's birth name but only the transgender name they've given you? What if they change their legal name? Aren't some names ambiguous with respect to gender? Perhaps consistent truth-telling would allow the use of an assumed name in some situations and not allow it in others. Your relationship to the individual certainly influences the wisest course. The more distant the relationship, the less responsibility you may have to pursue a confrontation when addressing them by name. The closer the relationship, the more you may have a duty to pursue such confrontations. In any case, we must always speak the truth in love when addressing a person by name.

2. Be at Peace with All People

Paul writes, 'If possible, so far as it depends on you, be at peace with all men' (Rom. 12:18 NASB). That means that offensiveness doesn't necessarily equal faithfulness. While offensiveness might be evidence of fidelity to the gospel, it might also be evidence that we are pugnacious. And we don't get brownie points for being angry jerks. The fool is the one who 'speaks rashly like the thrusts of a sword' (Prov. 12:18 NASB), but the wise 'ponders how to answer' (Prov. 15:28). The foolish person offends with his words. The wise person is persuasive, that his words might bring healing and life (Prov. 16:24).

When it comes to gospel witness, we need to build bridges wherever we can. And of course, that includes how we speak to and address sinners with our words. Paul modeled this for us at Mars Hill in Acts 17 and broke it down using simple terms in 1 Corinthians 9:22 where he explained: 'I have become all things to all men, so that I may by all means save some (NASB).'

Christians should not adopt the posture of a scold. If you can avoid conflict over pronouns and naming and still speak truthfully, then you are free to do so. Speaking to a co-worker directly normally doesn't require the use of gendered pronouns because 'you' is gender neutral. The difficulty comes when you speak about them. Even then, it may be possible to speak truthfully by employing a strategy of pronoun avoidance with the goal of building a relationship with your neighbor.

Watch

Follow along as you watch the video for Session 5.

This page is provided for you to take notes as you watch the video.

Group Experience

The Distinction between Male and Female is Social

Genesis 2 speaks to the social dimensions of male and female difference.

> Then the Lord God said, 'It is not good that the man should
> be alone; I will make him a helper fit for him.'
> So the Lord God caused a deep sleep to fall upon the man, and while
> he slept took one of his ribs and closed up its place with flesh. And
> the rib that the Lord God had taken from the man he made into
> a woman and brought her to the man. Then the man said,
> 'This at last is bone of my bones
> and flesh of my flesh;
> she shall be called Woman,
> because she was taken out of Man.'
> Therefore a man shall leave his father and his mother and hold
> fast to his wife, and they shall become one flesh. And the man
> and his wife were both naked and were not ashamed.
> **GENESIS 2:18, 21-25**

This text reveals that there is both sexual complementarity and gender complementarity embedded in God's good creation. To understand the difference between these two, we must understand the conventional distinction between sex and gender. Sex refers to one's biological organization for reproduction. Gender refers to the social manifestation of one's biological sex (see Ryan Anderson, *When Harry Became Sally*). Sex is a physical, bodily reality. Gender is a socio-cultural reality.

The spirit of the age is trying to tell us that the relationship between gender and sex is purely conventional and in no way essential. Increasingly, the dominant cultural narrative is that gender is a social-construct—that is, a set of customs and behaviors that one learns but which has no essential connection to biological sex. And that is why, many argue, some people's gender identity doesn't match their bodily identity. But is this what Scripture teaches? The answer is no.

In verse 18, the word 'helper' corresponding to Adam designates a social role for Eve within her marriage to Adam—a role that is inextricably linked to her biological sex. Adam's creation before Eve designates a social role within his marriage to Eve—a role that is inextricably linked to his biological sex. He is to be the leader, protector, and provider within this marriage covenant.

The implication of this teaching is that God has so made the world that there is a normative, holy connection between biological sex and gender identity. Notice that the social roles of the first man and woman in Genesis 2 are inextricably connected to their biological sex. The New

Testament reveals that these roles are not merely descriptive of the first marriage, but as normative for every subsequent marriage (1 Cor. 11:3; Eph. 5:21-33).

Moreover, the social order of the first family forms the foundation for leadership norms within the Christian church (1 Cor. 11:3-16; 1 Tim. 2:12-13). All of this presumes a normative connection between biological sex and social roles designed for that sex. It also presumes that a man understands himself to be a man and that a woman understands herself to be a woman. Self-identity and bodily identity match one another. There will be no transgender identities in the new creation. Men will know themselves as men, and women will know themselves as women, even though there is no marriage in the age to come (Mark 12:25; Luke 20:35).

The Distinction between Male and Female is Good

Paul reflected on the Genesis creation account in his words about false teachers in 1 Timothy 4:

> For everything created by God is good, and nothing is to be rejected if it is
> received with thanksgiving, for it is made holy by the word of God and prayer.
> **1 TIMOTHY 4:4**

Where does Paul get the idea that everything created by God is 'good'? Paul is simply reading Genesis 1 where it says throughout the six days of creation that God looked at what He had made and said that it was 'good' (Gen. 1:4, 10, 12, 18, 21, 25). And when God made the first male and female bodies, He said it was 'very good' (Gen. 1:31). And now Paul affirms that what was true about male and female design before the Fall is still true after the Fall. This means that even though God's good design in creation may be marred by the Fall and by sin, God's good design is not erased by the Fall and by sin.

What about Those Pesky Pronouns?

The pronoun (he/him, she/her) is a basic concept of grammar that we first learn as children by intuition. We might later have this concept cataloged by name in our elementary years, but not before we have a natural—if not subconscious—understanding of how and why we use certain pronouns for men that are different from those we use for women.

But today, the pronoun dominates so much of our cultural conversation. In the aftermath of the ongoing LGBTQ revolution, many have had to grapple with the 'preferred pronoun.'

Do we use someone's 'preferred pronoun' If It is incongruent with their biological sex?

What if we don't know someone's biological sex? Is it our duty to find out?

Are we lying when we call a biological male 'her,' or a biological female 'him' or 'them'?

Until very recently, most people didn't think twice about which pronouns to use, either for ourselves or for others. They came so *naturally*—in every sense of the word.

But the need for 'preferred pronouns' arises in a world that is captivated by several ideological commitments: 1) the separation of gender and sex such that these concepts are no longer mutually informing; 2) the questioning, if not outright rejection, of the male-female sexual binary; and 3) an atomization of the self that untethers self-concept from reality, such that one's self-determination defines human nature in ways that contradict the body's organization for reproduction.

At the heart of the phrase 'preferred pronouns' is a preference, the liking of one alternative over another. But whose preference? Is it God's? Or the individual's? Today, the 'preferred pronoun' centers the preference of the one being spoken about—regardless of whether he or she is being spoken to.

But what on the surface seems nothing more than polite deference could be indulging the self-destructive fictions of someone who needs help.

Traditionally, the pronoun is a statement of natural and categorical commonality that humanizes speech. It works at the level of the subconscious to connect and relate individual persons to other members of the human race. Today, as pronoun preferences multiply—theoretically as many and varied as there are people—each person becomes an alien 'other,' no longer associated by natural category.

Pronouns used to be simple and held in common. They reflected a common foundation that made community possible. Whether or not we are acquainted, I at least know any man on the street as a 'he,' sharing his manhood in common with every man born of woman. Familiar or not, I know any woman I meet as a 'she,' who shares her womanhood in common with every woman made from man. 'They' together form two halves of the human whole. When what is common is neglected or, worse, denied, the community suffers.

To return to our question above, should we use someone's preferred pronouns? If you are not aware of an incongruity between someone's biological sex and preferred pronouns, then we can't help but speak according to our knowledge. But we shouldn't contribute to the normalization of pronouns outside the 'he/him' 'she/her' binary. This is to undermine and cut against God's original creation of humanity as male or female. Occasionally, we may use 'they/them' pronouns when we are not sure, although this is a grey area.

What duty do we have to find out someone's biological sex? This depends on our relationship with the person. The closer and more intimate the relationship, the more responsibility one has to speak to the person according to the truth. A one-off acquaintance with a barista does not hold the same relational status as one's brother-in-law, for instance, and with different relationships come different levels of responsibility.

But when we do know the truth, we are to act according to it and not against it. This will sometimes mean having to speak in ways that contradict a person's chosen 'identity' in the form of pronouns.

How can we love our neighbors who are rejecting God's design?

Weekly Reflection

Main Points from Lesson 5:

In our fifth lesson, we have looked at God's design for male and female, recorded in Genesis. It is vital to understand that the difference between male and female is both biological and social. Furthermore, the distinction is good because God declared it to be so. Consider these main points from our lesson and discuss the application questions with your group.

1. Scripture affirms that there are only two sexes and therefore only two genders. Sex is a biological reality. Gender is a social reality. Sex refers to the body's organization for reproduction. Gender refers to the social manifestation of biological sex.

2. Genesis distinguishes male from female in the context of social characteristics and roles.

3. The distinction between male and female is good (1 Tim. 4:4). This is true before and after the Fall.

Knowing that the gender binary is a biological reality specifically designed by God, how can we respond to someone who argues that gender is fluid?

Some people argue that the relationship between sex and gender is purely conventional and in no way essential. Why is this a problematic belief?

In this week's lesson we discussed 'preferred pronouns.' Why is it not wise or advisable for Christians to use someone's preferred pronouns? Practically, how should we engage with someone who identifies as transgender?

This Week's Memory Verse

So God created man in his own image, in the image of God he created him; male and female he created them. [...] And God saw everything that he had made, and behold, it was very good.

GENESIS 1:27, 31a

Conversation Guide Session 5

What makes male and female different? Is it a biological thing, a self-concept, or something else altogether?

Males and females are different by God's design (Gen 1:27). Human males have XY chromosomes in every cell of their bodies, and females have XX. The Y chromosome directs male sexual development—external genitalia, testes, high levels of testosterone, etc. Females have XX chromosomes which direct their bodies to develop internal genitalia, a uterus, ovaries, and high levels of estrogen.

These differences are not only biological, but they are immutable. They cannot be changed or altered by surgery or therapy. Even if someone has a self-concept that doesn't align with their biological sex, this does not mean that they have a different biological sex. It simply means their mind is out of sync with their body. Sex is determined by biology, and gender is the outward expression of one's sex. The Bible does not make room for the conceptual untethering of gender from sex. A male is a man, and a female is a woman.

Is it destructive for a person to think of their biological sex as disconnected from their gender identity? In what ways?

Untethering gender from sex leads to the possibility of an infinite number of gender identities that are completely subjective and not grounded in reality. If gender and sex are disconnected, manhood and womanhood can no longer be objectively defined. If a man is not a male, what is a man? If a woman is not a female, what is a woman? If a male can be a woman, what does that mean? Is it a particular feeling? Or a particular experience? Or something else?

For all the differences there are among human cultures, they consistently have some way to signify male-female difference. They don't always signify those differences with the same customs, but they do by and large honor the difference in part by external presentation—especially how they dress themselves. That is why Deuteronomy 22:5 warns against blurring the ways that human cultures signify male-female difference: 'A woman shall not wear a man's garment, nor shall a man put on a woman's cloak, for whoever does these things is an abomination to the Lord your God.' Notice that the text does not define what a 'man's garment' or a 'woman's cloak' are. It merely tells us that men and women dress differently in part to signify their maleness or femaleness. Where human cultures in their own ways honor the distinction between male and female, we ought to affirm not blur those customs.

Biologically speaking, there are two sexes: male and female. If gender is the social manifestation of biological sex, our social expressions ought to honor and not obscure that male-female difference.

Should we use someone's 'preferred pronoun' if it is incongruent with their biological sex?

No. As Christians who are seeking to speak the truth in love, we should not use pronouns that are incongruent with someone's biological sex. Ephesians 4:25 says, 'Therefore, having put away falsehood, let each one of you speak the truth with his neighbor, for we are members one of another.'

What if we don't know someone's biological sex?

We can only speak the truth according to our knowledge of the truth. If we find out someone has a biological sex different from the gender they are presenting as, we should speak and act according to the truth. But if we do not know someone's biological sex, and we don't have any concrete reason to assume there is an incongruity between how they are presenting and their biological sex, we are certainly not duty-bound to find out. As Christians, we do not want to assume the worst but always assume the best. First Corinthians 13:4-7 is instructive here: 'Love is patient and kind; love does not envy or boast; it is not arrogant or rude. It does not insist on its own way; it is not irritable or resentful; it does not rejoice at wrongdoing, but rejoices with the truth. Love bears all things, believes all things, hopes all things, endures all things.'

Are we speaking truthfully when we call a biological male 'her,' or a biological female 'him' or 'them'?

No, we do not speak truthfully when we refer to someone as if they were something that they are not. We must speak the truth in love (Eph. 4:15).

How can we love our neighbors who are rejecting God's design?

We can love our neighbors by treating them as the image-bearers that they are. Our neighbors, regardless of their current embrace or rejection of God's design, are still valuable and have dignity— not because of their actions but because of who they are, bearers of the image of the Creator God. We can love our neighbors by acknowledging their dignity and worth through conversation, politeness, and gracious speech, but ultimately by sharing the truth with them.

A quote from famous atheist Penn Jillette can help illustrate this point:

> 'I've always said that I don't respect people who don't proselytize. I don't respect that at all. If you believe that there's a heaven and a hell, and people could be going to hell or not getting eternal life, and you think that it's not really worth telling them this because it would make it socially awkward—and atheists who think people shouldn't proselytize and who say just leave me alone and keep your religion to

yourself—how much do you have to hate somebody to not proselytize? How much do you have to hate somebody to believe everlasting life is possible and not tell them that? I mean, if I believed, beyond the shadow of a doubt, that a truck was coming at you, and you didn't believe that truck was bearing down on you, there is a certain point where I tackle you. And this is more important than that.'

While Jillette is talking about evangelism—and his point should be convicting to all Christians who have an opportunity to share the gospel and choose not to—the same point applies to the realm of gender and sexuality. If we believe God's Word and God's ways are not only true but also good for us, then isn't withholding this truth and goodness the opposite of love? Wouldn't that be hate?

We are not commenting on when is the right time to share, when is the right time to confront, etc. This will be up to the individual situation and relationship. Instead, we should aim to share the truth with our neighbors and pray God would use His Word and your witness to change hearts.

Week 6

INTERSEX

Individual Experience

Read this section before your group meets

In the last chapter, we looked at what the Bible has to say about transgenderism and gender dysphoria. In this chapter, we will consider the separate phenomenon known as intersex.

It is very important for readers to understand that the transgender experience is very different from the intersex experience. The transgender experience refers to people whose biological sex is not in question, although their so-called gender identity might be. Intersex refers to people who have experienced a physical disorder of sexual development (DSD). The term intersex does not refer to a single disorder. Rather, intersex is an umbrella term referring to the different ways that a person's physical sexual development can go off course. Oftentimes, intersex conditions result in the person's genital anatomy being ambiguous and not clearly revealing whether the person is male or female.

In the twentieth century, a physician named John Money pioneered a 'treatment' protocol for infants born with an intersex condition. That treatment protocol assumed that gender was a social construct and could be molded one way or the other by socialization. Money recommended that the parents and physicians choose a gender and then surgically reshape the baby's sexual anatomy to match that choice. The problem with this protocol is that it ignored the sex chromosomes of the infants, assuming that there was no connection between the child's biology and self-identity. As a result, many of the children who had undergone these surgeries grew up to feel themselves to be a different gender from what their parents had chosen for them. Sadly, many of the surgeries resulted in destructive changes that could not be reversed.

Some progressive theologians have claimed that intersex conditions are evidence that sex is not binary but a spectrum. In her book *Sex Difference in Christian Theology*, Megan DeFranza argues that the existence of people with intersex conditions calls into question the male-female binary revealed in Genesis 1 and 2. She suggests that Adam and Eve are 'progenitors' of human difference but not paradigms of such difference. Adam and Eve may manifest a sexual binary, but those two sexes must not be understood as the only two options. Indeed, she argues that in the new creation, there will be males, females, and others who are 'more than females or males.' Her approach calls into question the existence of the male-female binary.

Jesus's Teaching on the Male-Female Binary

What does the Bible teach us about intersex conditions? Obviously, the terms intersex or DSD do not appear in the Bible. Nevertheless, there is evidence that Jesus and the biblical writers knew of those born with conditions that we now refer to as intersex. Their knowledge of such persons does not lead them to abandon the male-female sexual binary that is taught in Genesis.

Matthew 19:1–12 stands as Jesus' longest and most sustained reflection on the nature and meaning of marriage. The Pharisees come to Jesus and ask whether Moses' law allows for divorce 'for any cause' (Matt. 19:3). Jesus answers by appealing to Genesis 1 and 2 and its teaching about the nature of marriage. In a rhetorical flourish, Jesus asks the Pharisees whether they had even read what Genesis 1 says, 'Have you not read that he who created them from the beginning made them male and female?' (v. 4; cf. Gen. 1:27). With this statement, Jesus affirms not only the sexual binary of the Genesis 1 creation account but also that marriage is defined as the covenanted union of one man and one woman.

Jesus also establishes a theological principle that affirms God's original design in creation as God's ongoing intention for His world. We can understand what is right and what is wrong by discerning what fits God's original design and what doesn't. Whereas the Pharisees were looking for a reason to rationalize easy divorce, Jesus wants them to know that 'from the beginning' it was not this way (vv. 4, 8). In other words, God originally designed marriage to be a covenant of one man and one woman before God. God designed that covenant to be permanent in this life because 'What God has joined together, let not man separate' (v. 6).

The logic is simple: If God's original design for marriage is permanence, then His design reveals His will for all marriages today. If God's original design includes the affirmation of a male-female binary, then His design reveals that the male-female binary is normative today. Any departure from that binary would be a consequence of the fallenness of creation, not of God's good design.

The Pharisees were not satisfied with Jesus' teaching about the permanence of marriage. They suggest that Jesus' teaching is at odds with Moses' divorce law and ask, 'Why then did Moses command one to give her a certificate of divorce and send her away?' (v. 7). Jesus explains that God provides Moses' divorce law because people are sinful and break their marriage covenants (v. 8). Nevertheless, anyone who divorces his wife, except for the cause of sexual immorality, and marries another commits adultery (v. 9). Jesus' disciples respond to His stringent teaching on marriage with the following statement: 'If the relationship of the man and his wife is like this, it is better not to marry' (v. 10 NASB). Jesus answers them, explaining:

> Not everyone can receive this saying, but only those to whom it is
> given. For there are eunuchs who have been so from birth, and there are
> eunuchs who have been made eunuchs by men, and there are eunuchs
> who have made themselves eunuchs for the sake of the kingdom
> of heaven. Let the one who is able to receive this receive it.
> **MATTHEW 19:11-12**

In the Ancient Near East, eunuchs were men who had been physically castrated so that they might serve in the court of the monarch. Their castration was considered a necessity due to the access they would have to the king's harem or other women in proximity to the king. These are the ones who Jesus says 'have been made eunuchs by men.' Those who had made themselves eunuchs for the kingdom likely were not physically castrated but had simply chosen not to be married for the sake of gospel ministry. But the ones who are eunuchs 'from birth' are likely those who are born with physical conditions that render them unable to have sexual relations—those who have what today are recognized as intersex conditions. Jesus knows about these dear people.

Disorder Does Not Nullify Order: Just the Opposite, It Testifies to It!

If you have followed the discussion to this point, you can see that anomalies in creation and nature do not erase creation or nature. In fact, in some ways, the only way we can spot an anomaly is if we have a concept of what is 'normal.'

Does it surprise you to learn that Jesus knew of gender and sexual anomalies?

As we said earlier, an intersex experience refers to the many different ways a person's physical sexual development can go off course. Do biological anomalies such as intersex undermine or reinforce God's original design in creation?

Life Application

The following is an excerpt from *What Is the Meaning of Sex?* (Crossway, 2013) by Denny Burk.

The phenomenon of intersex should call forth our compassion and our love for our neighbors who carry in their persons a painful reminder of the groaning creation. It should not call forth from us a revision of the binary ideal of Scripture. That binary ideal is the matrix from which a binary ideal of gender roles emerges as well.

How should parents deal with a child born with an intersex condition? There is no once-size-fits-all strategy, given the complexity of the possible conditions. Nevertheless, here are some guiding principles I would suggest for parents caring for a child with this condition. The first set of principles I would recommend are more theologically oriented. First, everyone needs to know what the creation ideal of Scripture is. According to Genesis 1–2, man's unfallen state is a clearly gendered state, and this is the norm. Second, the entrance of sin into the world and God's subsequent curse means that all kinds of physical difficulties afflict the human condition. Disorders of sex development would be included in that. Third, the gospel of Jesus Christ not only frees from the penalty and power of sin in the present, it also promises eternal life in the future. That life involves the resurrection of our physical bodies. It means a renewal and restoration of what was lost in the Garden of Eden. In the resurrection, all disorders of sex development will be swept away, and intersex people will be healed and made whole. That hope of restoration should be held out to the child throughout his life even if some ambiguities about his condition remain unresolved.

Here are some principles I would suggest with respect to medical treatments. First, parents should be extremely reluctant about—if not altogether against—corrective surgery when the child is an infant. This is especially the case when the surgery would involve the modification of the child's genitals or reproductive organs. Perhaps surgical procedures would be in order at some point during the child's life, but do not rush a child into surgery simply out of a desire to make the child 'normal.' Second, try to determine as soon as possible the chromosomal make-up of the child. If there is a Y chromosome present, that would strongly militate against raising the child as a female, regardless of the appearance of the genitals and other secondary sex characteristics. It would also suggest that medical treatments designed to make the child into a female are out of line. Third, understand that not all doctors and medical professionals share your biblical convictions.

Christians who encounter intersex conditions should consider how disorders in creation testify to God's creational order and respond by longing for the day when God will make all things new according to the gospel.

Watch

Follow along as you watch the video for Session 6.

This page is provided for you to take notes as you watch the video.

Group Experience

Implications of Jesus's Teaching

Christians have always affirmed the teaching of Genesis 1:27, which says,

> God created man in his own image,
> in the image of God He created him;
> male and female He created them.
>
> **GENESIS 1:27**

Jesus Himself reaffirmed the givenness of this binary in His remarks on divorce in Matthew 19:4. This distinction between male and female underlies the very fabric of biblical teaching about the nature of man. It is no small point to the Christian faith.

Questions remain, however:

How do people with intersex conditions fit into this binary?

Does their very existence call into question the legitimacy of the biblical binary between male and female?

Some theologians have argued that the existence of physical disorders like intersex calls into question the legitimacy of the Bible's teaching on the gender binary and would like to convince Christians to abandon the traditional understanding of texts like Genesis 1:27 and Matthew 19:4. Are they right?

Is the existence of intersex a defeater of the male-female paradigm?

The answer to this last question is a resounding 'no.' Intersex is not evidence of God's creative intention but of the brokenness that has entered creation as a result of the Fall. The original creational good of Eden is a male-female binary with all the reproductive capacity this design entails (Gen 1:28). Because of the curse, the entire cosmos (including our bodies) has been subjected to futility—to conditions such as cancer, Parkinson's, blindness, and, yes, even to intersex conditions (Rom 8:20, 23). However, these painful bodily maladies will not persist in the age to come; instead, they will be healed by it (Rev. 21:4).

But what of those who must endure painful and perplexing intersex conditions in this age?

What about Christians who are trying to figure out what discipleship looks like in an intersex body?

Although more can and should be said in answer to such questions (see Denny Burk, *What Is the Meaning of Sex*, 169-83), I would commend a few guidelines for thinking through this difficult issue as a Christian:

(1) We should agree with God that his original distinction between male and female is not just good but 'very good' (Gen. 1:31; cf. 1 Tim. 4:4). The spirit of the age is trying to convince us that the biological differences between male and female are of little consequence and can be safely ignored. What is primary is not one's bodily identity but their 'gender identity.' This point of view values self-expression more than God's revelation in nature and Scripture. This is the unbiblical logic of transgenderism (which must not be confused with intersex). But this is not a faithful way to think about God's world and our place in it. All of us must agree with what God says to be good. And in this case, the male-female binary is something that God affirms as 'very good.' We should, too.

(2) For people with intersex conditions, that means they should try to let God's revelation shine its full light on their situation. One thing that nature reveals is that the sexual binary doesn't begin and end in one's reproductive anatomy. It begins at conception when one's sex chromosomes come together as either XX (female) or XY (male). As one endoctrinologist says:

> It is the Y chromosome which determines the sex of the embryo as absence of a Y chromosome always results in the development of a female while even in the presence of multiple X chromosomes, the presence of a Y chromosome will result in the development of a male (Gard 1998: 133).

Because of this genetic reality, we should not ignore the chromosomal indicators of one's sex, even if an intersex condition has caused other physical ambiguities. Psychiatrist and urologist William Reiner was a researcher at the Johns Hopkins Children's Center, and he warns against treating persons with a Y chromosome as female (quoted in Melton 2001: 2110). Insofar as these binary indicators can be known, we should embrace them as indicators of God's good creative intention.

(3) When the underlying chromosomal situation is unknown or when there are other ambiguating factors, this is not an occasion for despair. In the very same text that Jesus affirms the male-female binary, He also acknowledges a category of persons who bear a striking resemblance to people with intersex conditions.

For there are eunuchs who were born that way from their mother's
womb; and there are eunuchs who were made eunuchs by men; and
there are also eunuchs who made themselves eunuchs for the sake of the
kingdom of heaven. He who is able to accept this, let him accept it

MATTHEW 19:12 NASB

A eunuch is someone who does not have the biological capacity for sexual relations 'either through a birth defect, castration, or a voluntary life of abstinence' (ESV Study Bible, p. 1861). What is clear is that Jesus knew of people who, through no fault of their own, were born with the inability to experience sexual relations and procreation. Nevertheless, this physical limitation was no limitation on their discipleship. When Jesus said these words, God had already revealed through the prophet Isaiah that devout eunuchs would receive an inheritance 'better than sons and daughters' (Isaiah 56:3–5). Indeed, one of the first Gentile converts to Christ was a eunuch (Acts 8:26–40).

What then about Gender Dysphoria?

How should we engage with those who experience painful and perplexing intersex conditions? What about Christians who are trying to figure out what discipleship looks like in an intersexed body?

The first thing to note as we address gender dysphoria is that we must make it clear that it is not the same thing as intersex. Intersex is a biological condition, whereas gender dysphoria is a psychological one.

What are we to do if we encounter thoughts and feelings that are out of line with one's body?

We must first recognize that such thoughts should not automatically be considered identity-forming. If we affirmed every thought or feeling that arose from our fallen natures, we would find ourselves quickly in a spiral of doom and despair or in a cloud of hedonistic futility.

But secondly, we must look to God's original design for our true identity and purpose. God created males for manhood and females for womanhood. In God's economy, there is no such thing as a female man or a male woman. By affirming the goodness of God's design in creation, we will be able to better see and appreciate God's purpose for making us male or female.

Tragically, too often the opposite drives people's gender dysphoria, having experienced some form of denigration of maleness or femaleness or some form of idolatrous elevation of what it means to be a man or a woman. Christians can show a better way by highlighting and celebrating the unique goodness of both manhood and womanhood.

Weekly Reflection

Main Points from Lesson 6:

In our sixth lesson, we have addressed disorders of sexual development that are often referred to as intersex conditions. Jesus' teaching in Matthew 19:1-12 affirms God's design for male and female as His ongoing intention for creation. His knowledge of people with conditions now referred to as intersex did not negate this truth. Instead of rooting our identity in our disordered sexual development, we are given a new identity in Christ. Consider these main points from our lesson and discuss the application questions with your group.

1. Jesus knew of those born with conditions that we now refer to as intersex, yet His knowledge of such persons did not lead Him to abandon the male-female sexual binary that is taught in Genesis.
2. Any departure from that binary would be a consequence of the fallenness of creation, not of God's good design.
3. Instead of depending on our feelings or what culture says, we should look to God's original design for our true identity and purpose.

How can we respond to the argument that intersex conditions are evidence that there are genders beyond male and female?

God set clear guidelines for gender and marriage in the beginning chapters of Genesis. How can we know that these guidelines apply to us today?

What would claiming your identity in Christ really look like?

This Week's Memory Verse

For everything created by God is good, and nothing is to be rejected if it is received with thanksgiving, for it is made holy by the word of God and prayer.
1 TIMOTHY 4:4-5

Conversation Guide Session 6

Does it surprise you to learn that Jesus knew of gender and sexual anomalies?

After the Fall in Genesis 3, the whole world was marred by the effects of sin and death. This is part of what Paul means in Romans 8:19-22:

> For the creation waits with eager longing for the revealing of the sons of God. For the creation was subjected to futility, not willingly, but because of him who subjected it, in hope that the creation itself will be set free from its bondage to corruption and obtain the freedom of the glory of the children of God. For we know that the whole creation has been groaning together in the pains of childbirth until now.
>
> **ROMANS 8:19-22**

Nothing in the world has been left untouched by the Fall—'creation was subjected to futility,' which includes 'bondage to corruption' (vv. 20–21). Theologians have long made the distinction between what is called natural evil and moral evil. A natural evil is something that does not function according to its pre-Fall design and causes harm, destruction, or disorder, such as hurricanes, earthquakes, or birth defects. In such cases, sin is not the direct cause of such evil but the indirect cause, which means there isn't moral culpability for such occurrences. Jesus makes this clear when He answers a question His disciples ask Him about a blind man in John 9:1–3:

> As he passed by, he saw a man blind from birth. And his disciples asked him, 'Rabbi, who sinned, this man or his parents, that he was born blind?' Jesus answered, 'It was not that this man sinned, or his parents, but that the works of God might be displayed in him.'
>
> **JOHN 9:1-3**

This man's blindness was not due to his or his parents' sin; rather, it was due to the effects of the Fall and what we would call a natural evil. Moral evil, on the other hand, is evil that is caused by human will or volition. This is what the Bible calls sin.

Jesus is God and knew about both natural and moral evil, and He knew that natural evil manifests in many different ways, including defects in sex formation.

How do people with intersex conditions fit into the male-female binary?

People with intersex conditions can be considered either male or female while having disordered or malformed sex characteristics that obscure their maleness or femaleness.

Does the very existence of intersex conditions call into question the legitimacy of the biblical binary between male and female?

No. Just as the existence of people who are born without arms does not create a new category of armless human, this person instead reflects a defect or disorder that is defined in terms that point to God's original design. 'Armless' points to God's original design of humanity with two arms. In the same way, people with intersex conditions do not erase the male-female binary. The very fact that we are able to say what is missing, or what is disordered, or what is malformed means that we have a concept of male and female that is the original design and measure of God's plan.

Is the existence of intersex a defeater of the male-female paradigm?

See the answer above.

But what of those who must endure painful and perplexing intersex conditions in this age?

Above all, we should love those with intersex conditions as persons made in the image of God. Everyone conceived and/or born of a woman—meaning every person on the planet, including the unborn—bears the image of God and thus makes him or her supremely valuable and dignified. People with an intersex condition are no different than those born with other conditions that may prohibit certain functions. These people should be loved and sympathized with and helped to embrace who they are as God's creatures and encouraged to hope for the day in Christ when all things will be made new. They should never be shamed because of their condition.

What about Christians who are trying to figure out what discipleship looks like in an intersex body?

We should encourage Christians with intersex bodies not to reject the male-female binary, but to learn about their own sex insofar as it can be determined. The presence or absence of a 'Y' chromosome will determine whether that person will develop testes or ovaries. The ability to produce small gametes (sperm) is only possible with a Y chromosome. The ability to produce large gametes (eggs) is only possible if the Y chromosome is absent. The church should incorporate people with these conditions into the life of the body and be a spiritual family to them—especially since there may be no possibility for marriage and children due to their condition. In Christ, we are one family—brothers and sisters who share a common faith, hope, and destiny after God makes all things new (Rev. 21:1–8).

Below are some verses to meditate on and encourage others with. Ephesians 2:19-22 talks about Christians' familial unity in the here and now:

> So then you are no longer strangers and aliens, but you are fellow citizens with the saints and members of the household of God, built on the foundation of the apostles and prophets, Christ Jesus himself being the cornerstone, in whom the whole structure, being joined together, grows into a holy temple in the Lord. In him you also are being built together into a dwelling place for God by the Spirit.
>
> **EPHESIANS 2:19-22**

First John 3:1-3 talks about Christians' familial unity awaiting God's renewal:

> See what kind of love the Father has given to us, that we should be called children of God; and so we are. The reason why the world does not know us is that it did not know him. Beloved, we are God's children now, and what we will be has not yet appeared; but we know that when he appears we shall be like him, because we shall see him as he is. And everyone who thus hopes in him purifies himself as he is pure.
>
> **1 JOHN 3:1-3**

Week 7
IDENTITY AND SANCTIFICATION

Individual Experience

Read this section before your group meets

'Who are you?'

It wouldn't be an understatement to say that this simple question, and the various ways it has been answered, gets to the heart of one of the most contested concepts today—the concept of identity.

There are almost limitless answers available to the question, 'Who are you?' This shows identity can be layered and multifaceted:

'I am a father.'
'I am a teacher.'
'I am a sister.'
'I am a Baptist.'
'I am a Christian.'
'I am Ben.'
'I am Jennifer.'

Identity is easier to recognize and harder to define, but we may begin with a simple definition: Identity is one's self-understanding or self-concept. This basic definition leads us to ask another, more fundamental question: Where does identity come from? Is it something we create? Or is it something we are given? How we answer this question, especially when considering what forms the core of our self-understanding, is the difference between a Christian and non-Christian account of the self.

The concept of identity is so contested and fraught today because of the rise of psychological challenges to traditional, historical understandings of the self. This history has been rehearsed thoroughly in Carl Trueman's excellent book, *The Rise and Triumph of the Modern Self*, but a brief summary may suffice here.

With the rise of philosophers such as Jean-Jacques Rousseau and Sigmund Freud and advances in technology that allowed humanity a semblance of control over nature, humanity's self and inner feelings began to take priority over our external relationships in determining how we thought of ourselves in the world. The result? Our society today is dominated by the idea of 'expressive individualism,' which is the assumption that our 'self' is constituted by our subjective feelings rather than external realities.

When we consider how our society talks about gender and sexuality today, we can see how psychological and technological changes serve to underwrite the discussion.

If a man says, 'I am a woman trapped in a man's body,' this statement prioritizes feelings over the body, nature, and reality.

If a woman says, 'I am a lesbian,' this statement prioritizes desire over design. While her body's sexual organs are quite literally oriented to a man's sexual organs, her feelings trump her body. Desire over design.

Of course, we only do this with what are 'socially acceptable' feelings. If someone who struggles with anorexia says they feel fat, nobody who cares about them will confirm their feelings. They will instead redirect them to facts about health and nutrition, even as they recognize the psychological complexity behind this eating disorder.

Five hundred or 1,000 years ago, some of the statements we affirm today would have been nonsensical—they quite literally would not have made sense. Tim Keller gives us a humorous example that illustrates the point:

> Imagine an Anglo-Saxon warrior in Britain in AD 800. He has two very strong inner impulses and feelings. One is aggression. He loves to smash and kill people when they show him disrespect. Living in a shame-and-honor culture with its warrior ethic, he will identify with that feeling. He will say to himself, *That's me! That's who I am! I will express that.* The other feeling he senses is same-sex attraction. To that he will say, That's not me. I will control and suppress that impulse. Now imagine a young man walking around Manhattan today. He has the same two inward impulses, both equally strong, both difficult to control. What will he say? He will look at the aggression and think, *This is not who I want to be, and will seek deliverance in therapy and anger-management programmes.* He will look at his sexual desire, however, and conclude, *That is who I am.*
>
> What does this thought experiment show us? Primarily it reveals that we do not get our identity simply from within. Rather, we receive some interpretive moral grid, lay it down over our various feelings and impulses, and sift them through it. This grid helps us decide which feelings are 'me' and should be expressed—and which are not and should not be. So this grid of interpretive beliefs—not an innate, unadulterated expression of our feelings—is what gives us our identity. Despite protests to the contrary, we instinctively know our inner depths are insufficient to guide us. We need some standard or rule from outside of us to help us sort out the warring impulses of our interior life
>
> And where do our Anglo-Saxon warrior and our modern Manhattan man get their grids? From their cultures, their communities, their heroic stories. They are actually not simply 'choosing to be themselves' – they are filtering their feelings, jettisoning some and embracing others. They are choosing to be the selves their cultures tell them they may be (Tim Keller, *Preaching: Communicating Faith in an Age of Skepticism* [Penguin, 2015], 135-36).

In other words, we need to be aware of how the prevailing culture is shaping our identities. Where we find our identities out of line with God's Word, we should opt to reform according to His Word.

This week, we are going to see how we can encourage our identities to be informed and reformed by God's Word and how we can help others do the same.

In this week's lesson, we are considering identity. What comes to mind when you think about your identity? How do we ensure that our identities are being shaped by God's Word and not the culture?

Life Application

We've all heard the term 'identity crisis.' What we may not know is that this term was first coined by German psychologist Erik Erickson in the twentieth century. The timing is no coincidence: as humanity became more introspective with the rise of modern psychology, identity crises abounded. But in one way, the concept of identity in crisis has been with humanity ever since we first asked the question, 'Who am I?' And the related question, 'Who do I want to be?'

All around us, our neighbors are experiencing identity crises. Some are genuinely struggling to know who they are or who they want to be. Others may be content with who they are now or who they want to be today, but tomorrow they may encounter something about themselves or the world that throws their perceived identity into crisis through self-doubt. Others think they know who they are but have never encountered the God who made them.

Questions of identity offer a ready segue for Christians who want to talk to their neighbors about their deepest hopes and fears. With the modern move away from external markers of identity, such as objective relationships, toward internal markers of identity, such as subjective feelings, there exist more occasions for people's self-concepts to change or to be built on an unsteady foundation. This reality should drive us to sympathy and compassion for those who may experience an identity crisis.

But the biblical worldview doesn't stop with sympathy and compassion. The biblical worldview grounds our own identities in something—Someone—more solid, and it helps us point others toward the same.

When Moses asked God His name in Exodus 3, he was asking after God's identity. Notice how God answers Moses in Exodus 3:14: 'I AM WHO I AM.' Who is God? He is. This is who God is: He is infinite, eternal, and unchangeable. As such, He is self-existing, meaning He has no beginning or end, and He gets His being, His identity, from Himself. As creatures, we cannot answer the same way—to do so would be blasphemous. We are different from God in that we derive our being from God—He is our Maker, our Creator.

This is what the psalmist confesses in Psalm 139:13-16:

> For you formed my inward parts; you knitted me together in my mother's womb.
> I praise you, for I am fearfully and wonderfully made. Wonderful are your works;
> my soul knows it very well. My frame was not hidden from you, when I was
> being made in secret, intricately woven in the depths of the earth. Your eyes
> saw my unformed substance; in your book were written, every one of them,
> the days that were formed for me, when as yet there was none of them.
> **PSALM 139:13-16**

The psalmist's words in Psalm 139 apply to everyone—our neighbors, our family, our friends. We are all fearfully and wonderfully made by God.

In a world increasingly obsessed with identity, we shouldn't be surprised when identity crises multiply. But God's Word gives us a better and more sure foundation and points us to better answers to the questions, 'Who am I?' and 'Who do I want to be?' I am fearfully and wonderfully made, and I can be a child of God through Christ.

In his book *Confessions*, Augustine makes this profound statement: 'You have made us for yourself, O Lord, and our hearts are restless until they rest in You.' We could say the same thing about identity: 'You have made us for yourself, O Lord, and our identities are restless until they rest in You.'

Let us find rest in God and help our neighbors to do the same.

Watch

Follow along as you watch the video for Session 7.

This page is provided for you to take notes as you watch the video.

Group Experience

What does the Bible say about identity?

The Bible presents an objective account of the world and everything in it, which includes who we are and what we were made for, which can and should ground identity.

If we are going to think of identity in a way that is informed by the Bible, we should look at how the Bible describes humanity. To do this, we should closely follow how the Bible unfolds human history from creation, fall, redemption, and new creation.

Creation

The Bible teaches us in Genesis 1 and 2 that humans are created in the image of God, male and female (Gen. 1:27–28). This is the most important aspect of our identity—that we are image-bearers of our Maker. God's image should ground our self-understanding and our self-worth. Importantly, this includes being created male or female. Both men and women are created in the image of God and are equal in value and dignity.

How should a biblical understanding of creation inform our identity?

Fall

The Bible also teaches us that in our earthly father, Adam, we all fell into sin and corruption, which means we bear the mark and effects of original and indwelling sin. This should ground our self-humility, especially as we consider how our particular sins may differ from our neighbor's.

How should a biblical understanding of the Fall inform our identity?

Redemption and New Creation

But praise be to God; humanity's fall into sin is not the end of the story. The Bible's central message is God's work in Christ in redeeming and renewing the lost who put their faith and trust in Him. When we unite ourselves to Jesus by faith, His objective life, death, and resurrection become our personal possession, which means we become sons and daughters of the Most High God. And at the resurrection, our bodies and the image of God that was marred by sin will be restored to their original nature (1 Cor. 15:12-58). Christian redemption gives our identities an already-but-not-yet quality, having been washed clean by the blood of Christ but still awaiting consummation and perfection. That is what theologians call sanctification.

How should a biblical understanding of redemption and new creation inform — or better yet, reform—our identity?

Christian Identity

This final element of identity has caused some division in the church, as some teachers have promoted the concept of 'Gay Christianity' for those who confess faith in Christ but who still experience same-sex attraction, or even 'Transgender Christians,' who similarly experience gender dysphoria even while they confess faith.

How should we think about a 'Gay Christian' or 'Transgender Christian' identity? Are these identities biblical? Is it appropriate for a Christian to claim these identities?

First Corinthians 6:9–11 can help us think through this question biblically. In these verses, Paul writes,

> Or do you not know that the unrighteous will not inherit the kingdom of God? Do not be deceived: neither the sexually immoral, nor idolaters, nor adulterers, nor men who practice homosexuality, nor thieves, nor the greedy, nor drunkards, nor revilers, nor swindlers will inherit the kingdom of God. And such were some of you. But you were washed, you were sanctified, you were justified in the name of the Lord Jesus Christ and by the Spirit of our God.
>
> **1 CORINTHIANS 6:9-11**

In this passage, Paul is writing to the church in Corinth, which was a body of believers composed of sinners saved by grace—the kind of sinners that Paul describes in this list of vices that includes homosexuality.

Notice what Paul makes clear: those who persist in such sins will not inherit the kingdom of God. That is a grave warning. It means they remain dead in their trespasses and sins and under the wrath of God. But did you catch what Paul said in verse 11? 'And such were some of you.'

That means that he was writing to a church full of people who used to practice such things, even to the extent that they 'were' such—their identity was 'sexually immoral,' or 'idolater,' or 'thief.'

But praise be to God; he didn't say 'are.' He said 'were'—such 'were' some of you. 'But' he continues, 'you were washed, you were sanctified, you were justified.' How? 'In the name of the Lord Jesus Christ and by the Spirit of our God.' In other words, their union with Christ by the Spirit of God meant that these believers were no longer identified by these sins but by something else.

Paul says it this way in 2 Corinthians 5:17:

> Therefore, if anyone is in Christ, he is a new creation. The
> old has passed away; behold, the new has come.
> **2 CORINTHIANS 5:17**

If you are a Christian, you are a new creation awaiting the new creation. The old man that fell in Adam is passing away, and the new man in Christ is here to stay. That is good news!

This is why taking on same-sex orientation or transgender as an identity category is problematic. From a Christian perspective, it invites us to embrace fictional identities that go directly against God's revealed purposes for His creation. It invites us to define ourselves and the meaning of our lives according to the sum total of our fallen sexual attractions.

But God's purposes for us are obscured if we make our sinful sexual attractions the touchstone of our being. God gives us a bodily identity that indicates His purposes for us sexually, and those purposes are unambiguously ordered to the opposite sex within the covenant of marriage. To embrace an identity that goes against God's revealed purpose is, by definition, sinful.

Christian, you are not your sin. You are not your temptation to sin. By the life, death, and resurrection of Jesus Christ, you have been set free. This doesn't mean that you won't have other identities beyond 'Christian'—you will still be mother, or father, or teacher, or from Lexington—and you will still struggle with temptation and sin. But at your core, you are a blood-bought believer. You are a Christian not defined by your failures or shortcomings that separate you from God but by Christ's perfection that brings you to God.

Weekly Reflection

Main Points from Lesson 7:

In our seventh lesson, we have looked at how God's Word informs and reforms our identities. Based on the proscriptions against certain sinful behaviors in 1 Corinthians 6, it would be unbiblical to ground our identity in something sinful. We are not our sin. Rather, we have been bought with a price and are made new, clothed in the righteousness of Christ. Consider these main points from our lesson and discuss the application questions with your group.

1. The Bible presents an objective account of the world and everything in it, which includes who we are and what we were made for. This account can and should ground our identity.
2. Constructing one's identity on something that the Bible declares is sinful is destructive. This includes homosexuality and transgenderism.
3. If you are a Christian, you are a new creation, and your identity is rooted in Christ.

How does the Bible's account of creation, fall, redemption, and restoration inform and ground our identity?

What implications does the Bible's teaching on identity have for the claims made by the LGBTQ movement? How can we speak the truth in love to people who identify with this movement?

Before you knew Christ, how did you form your identity? What changed when you became a Christian?

This Week's Memory Verse

Therefore, if anyone is in Christ, he is a new creation. The
old has passed away; behold, the new has come.
2 CORINTHIANS 5:17

Conversation Guide Session 7

What comes to mind when you think about your identity?

There isn't a wrong answer to this question, as we all have varying experiences and backgrounds that not only form our identities but also how we think about the concept of identity itself. Some people may think of identity primarily in terms of where they come from—their family, country, hometown, etc. Some may think of identity primarily in terms of what they do—their job, their career, their favorite hobby, etc. Some may think of identity primarily in terms of their relationships—husband, mother, sister, etc.

This is a good place to consider how identity is formed and how we contribute to our identity's formation. When someone asks the question, 'Who are you?,' what comes immediately to mind? What comes to mind on deep reflection? What things belong to the core of someone's identity, and what things are more at the periphery?

How do we ensure that our identities are being shaped by God's Word and not the culture?

Paul addresses this very question and concern in Romans 12:1-2:

> I appeal to you therefore, brothers, by the mercies of God, to present
> your bodies as a living sacrifice, holy and acceptable to God, which
> is your spiritual worship. Do not be conformed to this world, but be
> transformed by the renewal of your mind, that by testing you may discern
> what is the will of God, what is good and acceptable and perfect.
> **ROMANS 12:1-2**

According to Romans 12:2, we are not to be conformed to this world—its pursuits, values, or constructs. Instead, we are to be transformed. How? By the renewing of our minds. This transformation and renewal in Romans 12:2 comes by testing and discerning the will of God and pursuing what is good and acceptable and perfect, namely, pursuing what God says to pursue in His Word. We are transformed by reading and submitting to the Word of God.

Peter put it this way in 1 Peter 1:13-23:

Therefore, preparing your minds for action, and being sober-minded, set your hope
fully on the grace that will be brought to you at the revelation of Jesus Christ. As
obedient children, do not be conformed to the passions of your former ignorance,
but as he who called you is holy, you also be holy in all your conduct, since it is
written, 'You shall be holy, for I am holy.' And if you call on him as Father who judges
impartially according to each one's deeds, conduct yourselves with fear throughout
the time of your exile, knowing that you were ransomed from the futile ways
inherited from your forefathers, not with perishable things such as silver or gold,
but with the precious blood of Christ, like that of a lamb without blemish or spot.
He was foreknown before the foundation of the world but was made manifest in
the last times for the sake of you who through him are believers in God, who raised
him from the dead and gave him glory, so that your faith and hope are in God.
Having purified your souls by your obedience to the truth for a
sincere brotherly love, love one another earnestly from a pure
heart, since you have been born again, not of perishable seed but
of imperishable, through the living and abiding word of God.

1 PETER 1:13-23

Several commands in this passage point us away from worldliness, or worldly pursuits and
identities, and toward godliness, which includes godly pursuits and godly identities. Verse 13 says
to 'set your hope fully on the grace that will be brought to you at the revelation of Jesus Christ.'
Verse 14 says instead of conforming to passions—desires!—that you had when you were apart
from Christ, to 'be holy in all your conduct' (v. 15) and to do so in the fear of God (v. 17). What
is our motivation for holiness? The knowledge of the grace that we have received in Christ, having
been ransomed from futility and emptiness and death by our faith in Christ, which is based on the
foreknowledge of God and is the engine of our faith and hope. In other words, a biblical identity
is grounded in biblical knowledge that motivates biblical obedience.

How should a biblical understanding of creation inform our identity?

A biblical understanding of creation tells us several true things about ourselves that should ground
our identity: 1) We are created in the image of God, which gives us immeasurable dignity and
worth. 2) We are created male or female in the image of God, which tells us that being a man or
woman is not only part of God's original design and is good, but it is right and good that being
male or female is integral to who we are as image-bearers. In other words, being a man is good and
nothing to be ashamed of, and being a woman is good and nothing to be ashamed of. Embracing
our God-given sex is part of embracing a God-given identity. 3) Being created in the image of God
is part of what grounds our identity as God's crowning creation, but the commands God gives
the first man and woman also help us understand our purpose, which is part of our identity. In
Genesis 1:28, God gives man and woman what has come to be called the 'creation mandate':

> And God blessed them. And God said to them, 'Be fruitful and multiply and fill
> the earth and subdue it, and have dominion over the fish of the sea and over
> the birds of the heavens and over every living thing that moves on the earth.'
> **GENESIS 1:28**

The creation mandate supplies us with God-given purposes and God-endorsed aims and activities that can and should inform our identities. God tells the man and woman to be 'fruitful and multiply.' Getting married and having children is part of God's good design. Even if someone doesn't marry or have children, they can contribute to this good purpose by supporting and encouraging families—not only their own biological families but also families in the household of God. God also tells the man and woman to 'fill the earth and subdue it' and to 'have dominion' over the created world. Here is a God-given endorsement of work and labor that is creative, that brings order out of disorder, work that is constructive and beneficial and even lordly and commanding. Genesis 1 and 2 give us an entire theology of personhood, work, and identity, and as we saw in week 1, these chapters ground everything else the Bible says about God's will for humanity.

How should a biblical understanding of the Fall inform our identity?

When Adam and Eve fell into sin, the image of God that they were created in and bore was not completely erased, but it was effaced. The image of God was obscured in some ways and diminished because of their sin. In light of a biblical understanding of the Fall, our identities should be humble, not proud, and aware of our own tendencies toward sinfulness. As sons and daughters of Adam, we inherited a sinful nature that predisposes us to rebel against God.

This is Paul's verdict in Romans 3, where he gathers together and summarizes the Old Testament's teaching on the total depravity of human sinfulness:

> 'None is righteous, no, not one;
> no one understands; no one seeks for God.
> All have turned aside;
> together they have become worthless;
> no one does good, not even one.'
> 'Their throat is an open grave;
> they use their tongues to deceive.'
> The venom of asps is under their lips.'
> 'Their mouth is full of curses and bitterness.'
> 'Their feet are swift to shed blood;
> in their paths are ruin and misery,
> and the way of peace they have not known.'
> 'There is no fear of God before their eyes.'
> **ROMANS 3:10-18**

If you look at the cross-references in your Bible, you can see that these verses come from a number of different places in the Old Testament. This is the Bible's assessment of humanity apart from God's grace. This should not only make us humble but also patient with other sinners like us—this was Paul's attitude in 1 Timothy 1:15!

How should a biblical understanding of redemption and new creation inform—or better yet, reform—our identity?

Jesus came to make all things new. He came and lived a perfect life to give us His perfect righteousness; He died a sinner's death to pay the penalty of wrath that was owed our sin, and He rose from the grave to secure us a resurrection to eternal life. Jesus did not come to deal with the penalty of sin so that we could continue sinning. He came to set us free from sin and death.

Christians should form and reform their identities in this light, being formed and reformed by 'the grace of the Lord Jesus Christ and the love of God and the fellowship of the Holy Spirit' (2 Cor. 13:14).

The book of 1 John helps us understand the Christian's identity in light of Christ's finished work on the cross on our behalf and ongoing sanctification where sin remains in our lives, but sin that is being actively repented of and denied. Look at 1 John 1:5–10:

> This is the message we have heard from him and proclaim to you, that God is light, and in him is no darkness at all. If we say we have fellowship with him while we walk in darkness, we lie and do not practice the truth. But if we walk in the light, as he is in the light, we have fellowship with one another, and the blood of Jesus his Son cleanses us from all sin. If we say we have no sin, we deceive ourselves, and the truth is not in us. If we confess our sins, he is faithful and just to forgive us our sins and to cleanse us from all unrighteousness. If we say we have not sinned, we make him a liar, and his word is not in us.
> **1 JOHN 1:5-10**

This is the Christian's identity: sinner saved by grace. Not denying remaining sin but repenting of indwelling sin as God forgives us and cleanses us from all unrighteousness. Christian, after all, means 'little Christ.' As we are in Him by faith, we bear His righteousness, and God calls us His sons and daughters. Be who you are!

What about a 'Gay Christian' or 'Transgender Christian' identity? Are they biblical? Are they Christian?

A 'gay Christian' and 'transgender Christian' identity are out of step with how the Bible speaks about the new creation that God makes when someone passes from death to life by putting their faith in Jesus Christ. 'Gay' or 'transgender' may describe how someone identifies before they come to Christ, but in Christ, no one is 'gay' or 'transgender' any longer. They are new creations awaiting the new creation, even if the feelings of same-sex attraction or gender dysphoria are not miraculously removed immediately.

Even more concerning, someone who takes on a 'gay Christian' or 'transgender Christian' identity could be holding on to known sin instead of confessing it and repenting of it, or worse, denying that something is sinful that the Bible clearly calls sin. It is one thing to admit to a certain sin struggle or pattern of sin struggles while repenting of such sin. It is another thing to say that these sins are part of who you are in Christ. For this reason, we strongly discourage 'gay Christian' or 'transgender Christian' identities. These identities are an oxymoron; they are saying two opposite things.

1 John helps us again here. Look at 1 John 2:15–17:

> Do not love the world or the things in the world. If anyone loves the world,
> the love of the Father is not in him. For all that is in the world—the desires
> of the flesh and the desires of the eyes and pride of life—is not from
> the Father but is from the world. And the world is passing away along
> with its desires, but whoever does the will of God abides forever.
> **1 JOHN 2:15-17**

The desires of the flesh and eyes are not from the Father; Christ is from the Father. 'Gay' and 'transgender' are not from the Father; 'Christian' identity is. Do not separate what God has joined together, and do not join together what God has separated.

Week 8
SEXUAL SIN AND THE GOSPEL

Individual Experience

Read this section before your group meets

In this study, we have spent a lot of time learning what the Bible says about God's design and purpose for marriage and human sexuality. And if your heart has been open to the Scriptures, then at some point, you probably have been convicted of the ways you fall short of God's glory.

While it has been our aim to interlace each topic with God's grace in the gospel, we wanted to conclude by devoting an entire chapter to this theme—not as an appendix to an otherwise judgment-filled study, but as an emphatic punctuation, as a point of crescendo and climax.

You see, a Christian understanding of God's revelation, which includes God's moral law, should drive us to God's mercy and grace in the gospel. That is exactly what we see Paul doing in the first chapter of his letter to his son in the faith, Timothy:

> Now we know that the law is good, if one uses it lawfully, understanding this, that the law is not laid down for the just but for the lawless and disobedient, for the ungodly and sinners, for the unholy and profane, for those who strike their fathers and mothers, for murderers, the sexually immoral, men who practice homosexuality, enslavers, liars, perjurers, and whatever else is contrary to sound doctrine, in accordance with the gospel of the glory of the blessed God with which I have been entrusted.
> **1 TIMOTHY 1:8-11**

In these verses, the Bible teaches us that sexual immorality, which is here set alongside myriads of other sins that break God's moral law as summed up in the Ten Commandments, is not only contrary to sound doctrine but, even more, contrary to the gospel.

The Bible is clear that we are saved by faith alone through grace alone in Christ alone. Is Paul teaching something different in these verses (1 Timothy 1:8-11)?

What are the implications of Paul saying that these things listed are contrary to sound doctrine?

Here's part of what he means: If someone believes something isn't sinful that God's Word clearly labels as sin, then they are saying that they do not need Jesus to cleanse them of that sin, which means they are not made clean of it by repentance and faith.

If the Bible calls something a sin, is it loving or truthful to say that it is not a sin?

We don't preach the gospel by downplaying or diluting the Bible's teaching on sin, even sexual sin. Many false teachers have arisen in our day—just as in Paul's day—that preach a gospel contrary to the sound doctrine contained in the Scriptures. This is perhaps nowhere clearer in our day than with the Bible's teaching on sexuality.

Because gender and sexuality have become so central to identity and politics today, the temptation to downplay the Bible's teachings is perhaps no greater than in the areas of adultery, homosexuality, and gender identity.

But what does Paul do in 1 Timothy? He preaches the gospel by naming God's law for what it is, sin for what it is, and then pivoting right to the gospel.

Look at 1 Timothy 1:12-14:

> I thank him who has given me strength, Christ Jesus our Lord, because he
> judged me faithful, appointing me to his service, though formerly I was
> a blasphemer, persecutor, and insolent opponent. But I received mercy
> because I had acted ignorantly in unbelief, and the grace of our Lord
> overflowed for me with the faith and love that are in Christ Jesus.
> **1 TIMOTHY 1:12-14**

Do you see how Paul preached the gospel to Timothy? He numbers himself amongst the sinners in verse 13. This point is very important to consider! The apostle Paul, who wrote about a third of the New Testament, did not see himself as better than the sinners he just named in the previous passages. Just the opposite, in fact!

Read 1 Timothy 1:15-16:

> The saying is trustworthy and deserving of full acceptance, that Christ Jesus came
> into the world to save sinners, of whom I am the foremost. But I received mercy
> for this reason, that in me, as the foremost, Jesus Christ might display his perfect
> patience as an example to those who were to believe in him for eternal life.
> **1 TIMOTHY 1:15-16**

Did you catch that? Paul not only numbered himself among the sinners but also put himself first in line with the sinners! This is not the kind of line where first is best. No, first is worst—Paul calls himself the 'foremost' of sinners. That's a remarkable statement, given that he just listed 'those who strike their fathers and mothers, for murderers, the sexually immoral, men who practice homosexuality, enslavers, liars, perjurers.'

That is gospel humility, and it's the kind of humility that is commended in the Bible to those who believe that all are created in God's image, that all have fallen short of God's glory, and that all are made righteous solely on the basis of the merits and righteousness of another: Jesus Christ. That's where the gospel, the good news, comes in: Paul, as the chief of sinners, was given strength (v. 12), was judged faithful (v. 12), and received mercy and grace that overflowed with faith and love (v. 14) that led to eternal life (v. 16).

What better news in the world is there? This is where we want to conclude our study on gender and sexuality, with the good news that Jesus Christ came into the world to save sinners, of whom we are foremost.

We've considered in previous lessons the transforming power of the gospel. When someone comes to Christ, there is a transformation in identity. This was true in the first century, and it is true today. How does the gospel inform how we think about the issues and questions we've considered in our study?

Life Application

On March 21, 1858, Charles H. Spurgeon preached a sermon titled 'The Glorious Gospel.' His text was 1 Timothy 1:15. As we consider the gospel, meditate on the following excerpt from Spurgeon's sermon:

There is first of all, the Savior. And in explaining the Christian religion, this is where we must begin. The person of the Savior is the foundation-stone of our hope. Upon that person depends the usefulness of our gospel....

[Christ] is one so loving, so great, so mighty, and so well adapted to all our needs, that it is evident enough that he was prepared of old to meet our deepest wants. We know that Jesus Christ who came into the world to save sinners was God; and that long before his descent to this lower world, he was adored by angels as the Son of the Highest. When we preach the Savior to you, we tell you that although Jesus Christ was the Son of man...yet was he eternally the Son of God, and hath in himself all the attributes which constitute perfect Godhead. What more of a Savior can any man want than God? Is not he who made the heavens able to purge the soul? If he of old stretched the curtains of the skies, and made the earth, that man should dwell upon it, is he not able to rescue a sinner from the destruction that is to come?...

Oh, sinner, when we preach a Divine Savior, perhaps the name of God is so terrible to thee, that thou canst scarcely think the Savior is adapted to thee. But hear thou again the old story. Although Christ was the Son of God he left his highest throne in glory and stooped to the manger. There he is, an infant of a span long. See, he grows from boyhood up to manhood, and he comes forth into the world to preach and suffer! See him as he groans under the yoke of oppression; he is mocked and despised; his visage more marred than that of any other man, and his form more than the sons of men! See him in the garden, as he sweats drops of blood! See him in Pilate's chamber, in which he is scourged and his shoulders run with gore!...

On the bloody tree behold him! See him dying with agony too exquisite to be imagined, much less to be described! Behold him in the silent tomb! See him at last bursting the bonds of death, and rising the third day, and afterwards ascending up on high, 'leading captivity captive!' Sinner, thou hast now the Savior before thee, plainly manifested... Oh, could I bring him before you, could I now bring him here to show you his hands and his side, if ye could now, like Thomas, put your fingers in the holes of the nails and thrust your hand into his side, methinks you would not be faithless, but believing. This much I know, if there be anything that can make men believe under the hand of God's most Holy Spirit, it is a true picture of the person of Christ. Seeing is believing in his case. A true view of Christ, a right-looking at him, will most assuredly beget faith in the soul.

The transcript for the full sermon is available at spurgeon.org/resource-library/sermons/the-glorious-gospel.

Watch

Follow along as you watch the video for Session 8.

This page is provided for you to take notes as you watch the video.

Group Experience

Paul models gospel humility in the passages we looked at in 1 Timothy.

When we talk about issues surrounding gender and sexuality, we can easily fall into one of two tendencies. The first is to dismiss sins connected to sexuality because they are uncomfortable to address or too personal, or perhaps because we know someone caught up in one of these sins and are afraid of not being able to lovingly relate to them if we speak truthfully and forthrightly. The second tendency is to so emphasize gender and sexual sins—especially the ones that we don't personally struggle with—that we begin to think and act like the Pharisee who looked at the tax collector and shook his head, saying:

> 'God, I thank you that I am not like other men, extortioners,
> unjust, adulterers, or even like this tax collector.'
> **LUKE 18:11**

The Bible is clear that this is not a righteous attitude. The other part of this tendency is to place sins related to sexuality in a category of their own such that they seem beyond redemption. This couldn't be further from the truth, as Paul demonstrated in 1 Timothy.

What is your tendency? Is it to downplay sexual sins or overplay them?

How can we keep from falling into either one of these tendencies?

The Bible gives the perfect antidote against downplaying or overplaying any certain sins: the gospel!

Think about it: at the cross of Christ, God's judgment against sin and God's mercy toward sinners meet! This is exactly what we see at the heart of one of the most important chapters in the Bible, Romans 3:23-26:

> For all have sinned and fall short of the glory of God, and are justified by his
> grace as a gift, through the redemption that is in Christ Jesus, whom God put
> forward as a propitiation by his blood, to be received by faith. This was to
> show God's righteousness, because in his divine forbearance he had passed
> over former sins. It was to show his righteousness at the present time, so
> that he might be just and the justifier of the one who has faith in Jesus.
> **ROMANS 3:23-26**

Did you see that? God is the just and justifier at the cross: punishing sins because they are gravely serious but dispensing mercy in justifying—declaring righteous—sinners because of His great love.

This message is the heartbeat of the church, and it should be the heartbeat of our ministries as well.

Not 'Heterosexuality' or 'Cisgender' but Jesus

In a world full of rebellion against our Creator, there is no shortage of brokenness to address—whether in our own lives or the lives of our neighbors. It is important as we address the brokenness and sin that comes from our fallenness in areas related to gender and sexuality that we don't hold up heterosexuality as the answer to homosexuality or cisgender as the answer to transgender.

The call to turn away from homosexuality or transgenderism in repentance is, first and foremost, a call to turn to Christ Jesus, not a call to turn toward 'normality.' Hell will be full of 'heterosexual' and 'cisgender' people who never repented of their sins or put their faith in Christ. No, the answer to sexual sin is repentance and faith in Christ.

Paul says it this way in 1 Corinthians 6:18-20:

> Flee from sexual immorality. Every other sin a person commits is outside the body, but the sexually immoral person sins against his own body. Or do you not know that your body is a temple of the Holy Spirit within you, whom you have from God? You are not your own, for you were bought with a price. So glorify God in your body.
> **1 CORINTHIANS 6:18-20**

Fleeing from sexual immorality is a command, which means it is necessary. We can't deny that the gospel includes a call to repentance. But notice that Paul's main emphasis here is aimed at addressing the heart. His call is for us to relinquish control over our own lives in recognition that we belong to God. This, after all, is the fundamental sin that needs to be repented of: pride (cf. Rom. 1). Once we turn from ourselves to God, though, we are called to 'be who you are,' which is a dwelling place of the Holy Spirit whose aim is to bring glory to God.

Be Who You Are in Christ

Christian freedom is proclaimed in the Christian gospel: freedom from sin, freedom from death, and ultimately freedom from the disorder and chaos that is downstream from both. Galatians 2:20 is definitive:

> I have been crucified with Christ. It is no longer I who live, but Christ who lives in me. And the life I now live in the flesh I live by faith in the Son of God, who loved me and gave himself for me.
> **GALATIANS 2:20**

This aim and hope are yours in Christ Jesus when you put your faith in Him, who loved you and gave Himself up for you.

So, we conclude our study with the gospel, which is a message of hope. This good news is for all, because God 'desires all people to be saved and to come to the knowledge of the truth' (1 Tim. 2:4).

This is the message that was entrusted to Paul, the reason he says he was appointed a preacher and an apostle (1 Tim. 2:7). It was to share the good news that 'there is one God, and there is one mediator between God and men, the man Christ Jesus, who gave himself as a ransom for all' (1 Tim. 2:5–6).

And we minister this gospel when we point others to Christ Jesus, by whom and for whom all things were created (Col. 1:16)—including us who were made male or female for His glory.

Amen.

How can the message of the gospel help us be better ministers of God's grace to all people?

Weekly Reflection

Main Points from Lesson 8:

In our eighth and final lesson, we focused on the gospel and what it means for our brokenness. None of us are immune from the total depravity of our sinful nature. The only remedy is repenting of our sins and trusting in Christ. The gospel is sufficient. Consider these main points from our lesson and discuss the application questions with your group.

1. When someone comes to Christ, there is a transformation of identity.
2. The ultimate goal is not heterosexuality or identifying as 'cisgender,' but knowing Christ.
3. The gospel is good news for all people; it proclaims freedom from the disorder and chaos that is the natural end of enslavement to our sinful nature.

Why is it destructive and antithetical to the gospel to affirm sin as permissible?

On the other hand, what is the effect of condemning some sins, such as homosexuality, as worse than others?

How does the gospel stand in contrast to all worldly attempts to free us from the effects of sin? Why is nothing else sufficient?

This Week's Memory Verse

The saying is trustworthy and deserving of full acceptance, that Christ Jesus came into the world to save sinners, of whom I am the foremost. But I received mercy for this reason, that in me, as the foremost, Jesus Christ might display his perfect patience as an example to those who were to believe in him for eternal life.
1 TIMOTHY 1:15-16

Conversation Guide Session 8

The Bible is clear that we are saved by faith alone through grace alone in Christ alone. Is Paul teaching something different in these verses?

Here are a few of the places in the Bible that teach salvation is by faith alone through grace alone in Christ alone:

> For we hold that one is justified by faith apart from works of the law.
> **ROMANS 3:28**

To be 'justified' in Romans 3:28 is to be declared and counted righteous. We are counted as such not because of anything we have done but because of what Jesus has done for us. Paul makes this clear in Romans 5:1–2:

> Therefore, since we have been justified by faith, we have peace with God through
> our Lord Jesus Christ. Through him we have also obtained access by faith into
> this grace in which we stand, and we rejoice in hope of the glory of God.
> **ROMANS 5:1-2**

Our faith in Christ is what justifies us, it's what gives us peace with God, and it's what grants us access to the grace and hope and glory of God. What a truth and treasure!

Ephesians 2:8-9 is also clear about the role of faith in salvation:

> For by grace you have been saved through faith. And this is not your own
> doing; it is the gift of God, not a result of works, so that no one may boast.
> **EPHESIANS 2:8-9**

The message here is clear: Salvation comes through faith in Christ, which is a gift of God and is the opposite of 'works'—meaning we cannot earn our salvation, we only receive it by faith. Verse 10 shows us how our Christian 'works' or obedience are the result of saving faith, not the cause of it:

> For we are his workmanship, created in Christ Jesus for good works,
> which God prepared beforehand, that we should walk in them.
> **EPHESIANS 2:10**

Ephesians 2:8–10 helps us see how calls to holiness in the Bible are not antithetical to the gospel but do belong in their proper place. Christians are called to put their faith in action in obedience. Non-Christians are called first to repentance and faith.

This is why Paul's teaching in 1 Timothy does not contradict the Bible's teaching about faith in salvation. For one, Scripture is perfect and holy (2 Tim. 3:16) and thus does not contradict itself. We interpret Scripture by Scripture, so Paul's teaching in Ephesians and Romans informs how we should read 1 Timothy and vice versa. Those who will not inherit the kingdom of God are those who remain in their sins because they never came to Christ by faith for salvation and cleansing from sin.

What are the implications of Paul saying that these things listed are contrary to sound doctrine?

Paul's description of the vice list in 1 Timothy 1:8-11 as that which is contrary to sound doctrine has massive implications for the way we should approach the Bible's teaching on sin, especially the Bible's teaching on sexual sin. Those who downplay or dismiss the Bible's teaching about sin—either by affirming something the Bible calls sin or ignoring it altogether—are teaching contrary to sound doctrine, which Paul connects to the gospel in this passage. This is a very grave warning. Those who deny that homosexuality or transgenderism are sinful are leading people away from the gospel and must be opposed. The same goes for anyone who says something isn't sinful that the Bible calls sin. If someone were to come along and say the Bible permits stealing, that person should be called out and opposed. Today, many so-called Christian teachers are saying that the Bible does not condemn homosexuality or transgenderism. The implications from 1 Timothy 1 are clear: these people are teaching contrary to sound doctrine.

If the Bible calls something a sin, is it loving or truthful to say that it is not a sin?

This question seems rhetorical on its face, but our culture's definition of love has made this question a legitimate one, at least in practice. Our culture says you cannot love someone if you don't affirm them, and this affirmation often is tied up with their lifestyle or choices. But the Bible's definition of love is different: Love 'does not rejoice at wrongdoing, but rejoices with the truth' (1 Cor. 13:6).

The Bible's definition of love makes it clear that if the Bible calls something a sin, it is not loving to tell someone it is not a sin. That would be the opposite of loving; it would be hateful. But this is where the gospel should free us to tell the truth. When we say something is sinful, we aren't saying it is hopeless. Just the opposite! We are saying that sin keeps a person from God, but God sent His Son to address sin and its penalty in order to bring us to God! Highlighting sin in humility, like Paul did, acknowledging our own sinfulness, is a loving act as we point people to God's grace.

What is your tendency? Is it to downplay sexual sins, or overplay them? How can we keep from falling into either one of these tendencies?

In today's culture, LGBTQ issues are prominent and seem to be everywhere. This is partly by design, as our culture seeks to normalize and destigmatize practices and behaviors championed by the LGBTQ community. Because of this ubiquity, it can be easy for the church to focus too much on sexual sins and neglect others, especially those that we are more prone to struggle with. The opposite may happen as well. Some in the church may try to avoid addressing sexual sins altogether because they know it is a point of contention in the culture and may think it will diminish their opportunities to minister to all people.

Both approaches are wrong and unbiblical. The Bible's emphasis on the sinfulness of humanity, the wrath due sin, and the graciousness of God's mercy in Christ to save us from sin and death should help us keep the gospel central to the mission of the church and our lives as Christians. We should not shy away from addressing sin, and when we address sin, we should not neglect addressing what Jerry Bridges has called the 'respectable sins' and those sins we struggle with. Remember, Paul lists lying right alongside homosexuality in 1 Timothy 1. This is sobering. All sin is rebellion against God, which means all sin must be repented of and laid at the foot of the cross. There, at the foot of the cross, we are all on level ground and cannot look down our noses at each other because we are prostrate before our Savior. That's a good place to be.

How can the message of the gospel help us be better ministers of God's grace to all people?

The message of the gospel reminds us that we are sinners saved by grace, and God 'desires all people to be saved and to come to the knowledge of the truth' (1 Tim. 2:4), 'not wishing that any should perish, but that all should reach repentance' (2 Pet 3:9)—even those in the LGBTQ community.

Appendix
THE NASHVILLE STATEMENT

This book is based on the theological perspective of The Nashville Statement, a Christian confessional statement released by the Council on Biblical Manhood and Womanhood in 2017. The statement is the work of more than eighty evangelical theologians and leaders who met in Nashville in August of 2017 to finalize a biblical statement of conviction concerning marriage, sexuality, and gender identity. Since its release, the Nashville Statement has received over 25,000 signatures and has been adopted by Christian churches and institutions across the world. The Nashville Statement is printed in full below.

NASHVILLE
STATEMENT
A COALITION FOR BIBLICAL SEXUALITY

"Know that the LORD Himself is God;
It is He who has made us, and not we ourselves..."
- Psalm 100:3

Preamble

Evangelical Christians at the dawn of the twenty-first century find themselves living in a period of historic transition. As Western culture has become increasingly post-Christian, it has embarked upon a massive revision of what it means to be a human being. By and large the spirit of our age no longer discerns or delights in the beauty of God's design for human life. Many deny that God created human beings for his glory, and that his good purposes for us include our personal and physical design as male and female. It is common to think that human identity as male and female is not part of God's beautiful plan, but is, rather, an expression of an individual's autonomous preferences. The pathway to full and lasting joy through God's good design for his creatures is thus replaced by the path of shortsighted alternatives that, sooner or later, ruin human life and dishonor God.

This secular spirit of our age presents a great challenge to the Christian church. Will the church of the Lord Jesus Christ lose her biblical conviction, clarity, and courage, and blend into the spirit of the age? Or will she hold fast to the word of life, draw courage from Jesus, and unashamedly proclaim his way as the way of life? Will she maintain her clear, counter-cultural witness to a world that seems bent on ruin?

We are persuaded that faithfulness in our generation means declaring once again the true story of the world and of our place in it—particularly as male and female. Christian Scripture teaches that there is but one God who alone is Creator and Lord of all. To him alone, every person owes glad-hearted thanksgiving, heart-felt praise, and total allegiance. This is the path not only of glorifying God, but of knowing ourselves. To forget our Creator is to forget who we are, for he made us for himself. And we cannot know ourselves truly without truly knowing him who made us. We did not make ourselves. We are not our own. Our true identity, as male and female persons, is given by God. It is not only foolish, but hopeless, to try to make ourselves what God did not create us to be.

We believe that God's design for his creation and his way of salvation serve to bring him the greatest glory and bring us the greatest good. God's good plan provides us with the greatest freedom. Jesus said he came that we might have life and have it in overflowing measure. He is for us and not against us. Therefore, in the hope of serving Christ's church and witnessing publicly to the good purposes of God for human sexuality revealed in Christian Scripture, we offer the following affirmations and denials.

Article 1

WE AFFIRM that God has designed marriage to be a covenantal, sexual, procreative, lifelong union of one man and one woman, as husband and wife, and is meant to signify the covenant love between Christ and his bride the church.

WE DENY that God has designed marriage to be a homosexual, polygamous, or polyamorous relationship. We also deny that marriage is a mere human contract rather than a covenant made before God.

Article 2

WE AFFIRM that God's revealed will for all people is chastity outside of marriage and fidelity within marriage.

WE DENY that any affections, desires, or commitments ever justify sexual intercourse before or outside marriage; nor do they justify any form of sexual immorality.

Article 3

WE AFFIRM that God created Adam and Eve, the first human beings, in his own image, equal before God as persons, and distinct as male and female.

WE DENY that the divinely ordained differences between male and female render them unequal in dignity or worth.

Article 4

WE AFFIRM that divinely ordained differences between male and female reflect God's original creation design and are meant for human good and human flourishing.

WE DENY that such differences are a result of the Fall or are a tragedy to be overcome.

Article 5

WE AFFIRM that the differences between male and female reproductive structures are integral to God's design for self-conception as male or female.

WE DENY that physical anomalies or psychological conditions nullify the God-appointed link between biological sex and self-conception as male or female.

Article 6

WE AFFIRM that those born with a physical disorder of sex development are created in the image of God and have dignity and worth equal to all other image-bearers. They are acknowledged by our Lord Jesus in his words about "eunuchs who were born that way from their mother's womb." With all others they are welcome as faithful followers of Jesus Christ and should embrace their biological sex insofar as it may be known.

WE DENY that ambiguities related to a person's biological sex render one incapable of living a fruitful life in joyful obedience to Christ.

Article 7

WE AFFIRM that self-conception as male or female should be defined by God's holy purposes in creation and redemption as revealed in Scripture.

WE DENY that adopting a homosexual or transgender self-conception is consistent with God's holy purposes in creation and redemption.

Article 8

WE AFFIRM that people who experience sexual attraction for the same sex may live a rich and fruitful life pleasing to God through faith in Jesus Christ, as they, like all Christians, walk in purity of life.

WE DENY that sexual attraction for the same sex is part of the natural goodness of God's original creation, or that it puts a person outside the hope of the gospel.

Article 9

WE AFFIRM that sin distorts sexual desires by directing them away from the marriage covenant and toward sexual immorality—a distortion that includes both heterosexual and homosexual immorality.

WE DENY that an enduring pattern of desire for sexual immorality justifies sexually immoral behavior.

Article 10

WE AFFIRM that it is sinful to approve of homosexual immorality or transgenderism and that such approval constitutes an essential departure from Christian faithfulness and witness.

WE DENY that the approval of homosexual immorality or transgenderism is a matter of moral indifference about which otherwise faithful Christians should agree to disagree.

Article 11

WE AFFIRM our duty to speak the truth in love at all times, including when we speak to or about one another as male or female.

WE DENY any obligation to speak in such ways that dishonor God's design of his image-bearers as male and female.

Article 12

WE AFFIRM that the grace of God in Christ gives both merciful pardon and transforming power, and that this pardon and power enable a follower of Jesus to put to death sinful desires and to walk in a manner worthy of the Lord.

WE DENY that the grace of God in Christ is insufficient to forgive all sexual sins and to give power for holiness to every believer who feels drawn into sexual sin.

Article 13

WE AFFIRM that the grace of God in Christ enables sinners to forsake transgender self-conceptions and by divine forbearance to accept the God-ordained link between one's biological sex and one's self-conception as male or female.

WE DENY that the grace of God in Christ sanctions self-conceptions that are at odds with God's revealed will.

Article 14

WE AFFIRM that Christ Jesus has come into the world to save sinners and that through Christ's death and resurrection forgiveness of sins and eternal life are available to every person who repents of sin and trusts in Christ alone as Savior, Lord, and supreme treasure.

WE DENY that the Lord's arm is too short to save or that any sinner is beyond his reach.

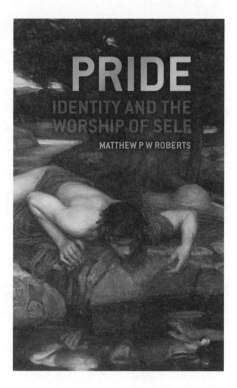

PRIDE

Identity and the Worship of Self

Matthew P. W. Roberts

- We are defined by who we worship
- Divide between duty and desire
- Redemption of identity

Our culture is obsessed with identity and it has been the cause of tense interaction with (and within) the Church. Rather than being a new challenge to the Christian faith, however, the identity issue is a very old one; it is fundamentally one of idolatry. Who we are, who we think we are, and how God in Christ restores our knowledge of ourselves in covenant with Him, are central biblical themes. But these things will only appear with clarity if we have the courage to tackle the idolatries of our own age at the root, and stand true to our calling as Christians to worship God and Him alone.

ISBN: 978-1-5271-0939-1

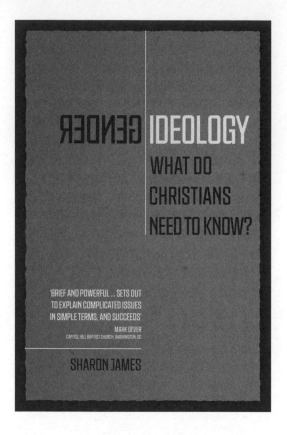

Gender Ideology

What Do Christians Need to Know?

Sharon James

- Equipping Christians to deal with transgenderism
- Defines and explains the subject
- Rebuts issues with the Christian worldview

The world has embraced the idea that gender is something that can be decided by individuals. As Christians encounter colleagues, friends and family members who identify as a gender other than the one they were born, we need to be informed and equipped with knowledge about what the issues are, what different terms mean and what the Bible has to say about these things. While we walk the line between loving our neighbour and not buying into the world's lies, Sharon James helps us in this informative and practical guide.

ISBN: 978-1-5271-0481-5

The Council on Biblical Manhood & Womanhood (CBMW) exists to spread the theological vision of the Danvers and Nashville Statements, which affirm the special and distinct design of male and female image-bearers and their callings in marriage and the church. CBMW publishes a theological journal titled *Eikon*, which is available for free along with hundreds of other resources at CBMW.org.

Family Research Council's mission is to advance faith, family, and freedom in public policy and the culture from a biblical worldview.

Founded in 1983, Family Research Council is a non-profit research and educational organization dedicated to articulating and advancing a family-centered philosophy of public life. In addition to providing policy research and analysis for the legislative, executive, and judicial branches of the federal government, FRC seeks to inform the news media, the academic community, business leaders, and the general public about family issues that affect the nation. In 2021, FRC launched the Center for Biblical Worldview to equip Christians with a biblical worldview and train them to advance and defend the faith in their families, communities, and the public square.

Visit FRC online at FRC.org. The Center for Biblical Worldview is online at FRC.org/worldview.

Christian Focus Publications

Our mission statement –

STAYING FAITHFUL
In dependence upon God we seek to impact the world through literature faithful to His infallible Word, the Bible. Our aim is to ensure that the Lord Jesus Christ is presented as the only hope to obtain forgiveness of sin, live a useful life and look forward to heaven with Him.

Our books are published in four imprints:

CHRISTIAN FOCUS

Popular works including biographies, commentaries, basic doctrine and Christian living.

CHRISTIAN HERITAGE

Books representing some of the best material from the rich heritage of the church·

MENTOR

Books written at a level suitable for Bible College and seminary students, pastors, and other serious readers. The imprint includes commentaries, doctrinal studies, examination of current issues and church history.

CF4•K

Children's books for quality Bible teaching and for all age groups: Sunday school curriculum· puzzle and activity books; personal and family devotional titles· biographies and inspirational stories – because you are never too young to know Jesus!

Christian Focus Publications Ltd,
Geanies House, Fearn, Ross-shire,
IV20 1TW, Scotland, United Kingdom.
www.christianfocus.com